C. E. Schumacher

The Jaulân

C. E. Schumacher

The Jaulân

ISBN/EAN: 9783741118050

Manufactured in Europe, USA, Canada, Australia, Japa

Cover: Foto ©Lupo / pixelio.de

Manufactured and distributed by brebook publishing software
(www.brebook.com)

C. E. Schumacher

The Jaulân

*Surveyed for the German Society for the Exploration of
the Holy Land,*

BY

SCHUMACHER, C.E.

Author of " Across the Jordan."

Translated, by permission, from the Transactions of the German Society.

WITH ALL THE ORIGINAL MAPS AND ILLUSTRATIONS.

LONDON :
ALEXANDER P. WATT, 2, PATERNOSTER SQUARE.

1888.

Wâdy el 'Ajam

UNSURVEYED

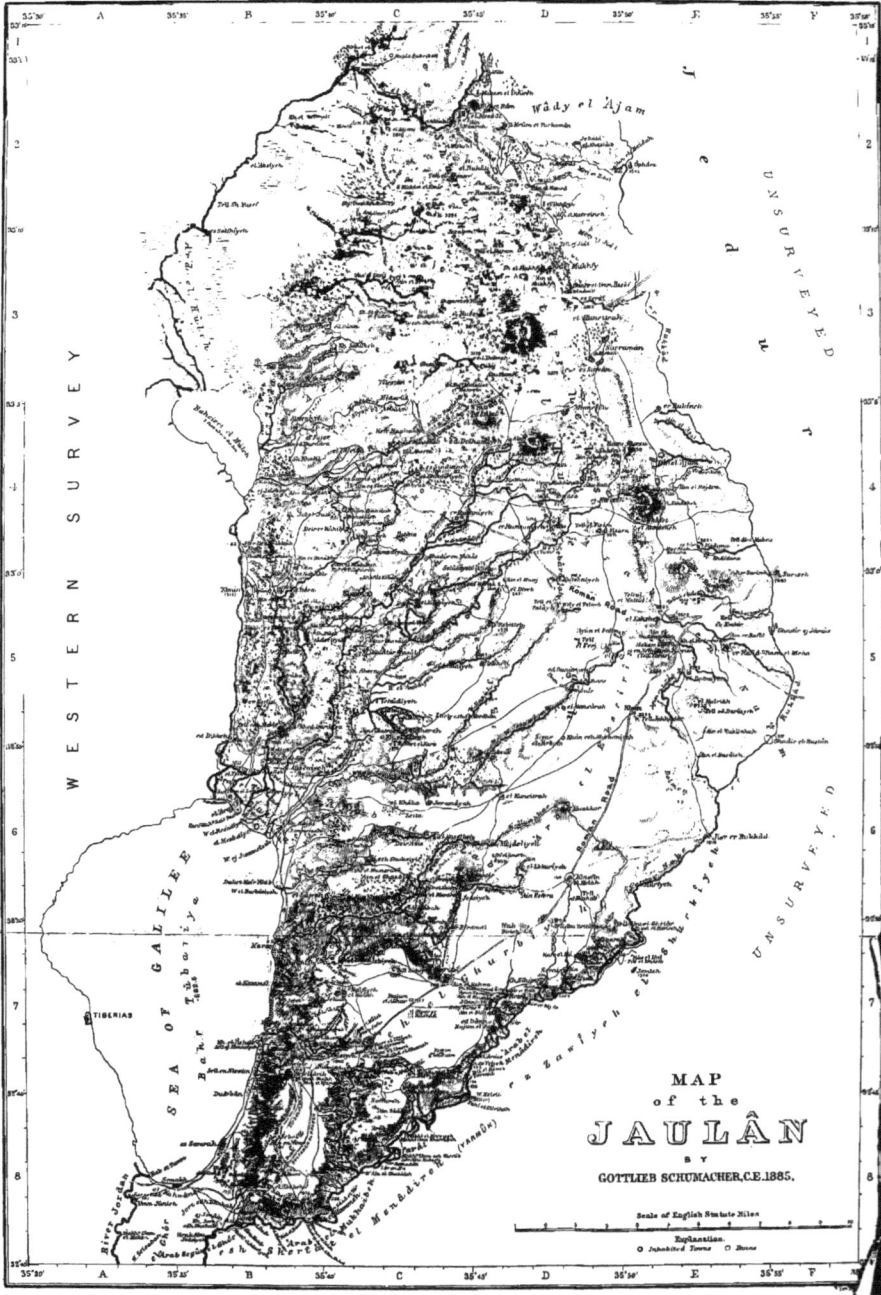

WESTERN SURVEY

SEA OF GALILEE

TIBERIAS

UNSURVEYED

River Jordan

MAP
of the
JAULÂN
BY
GOTTLIEB SCHUMACHER, C.E. 1885.

Scale of English Statute Miles

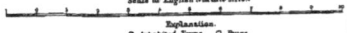

Explanation.
○ Inhabited Towns   ○ Ruins

PREFACE.

THIS work is translated from the *Zeitschrift* of the German Society for the Exploration of the Holy Land. We have to acknowledge with gratitude the permission accorded by the Committee of that Society to translate and reproduce the work with all its original illustrations. It will be found a worthy pendant to Captain Conder's works. The notes are mostly those furnished by Prof. Socin for the original edition. The spelling has been chiefly conformed to the usual practice in the published works of the Fund.

1, ADAM STREET, ADELPHI,
   March, 1888.

CONTENTS.

———•———

LIST OF ILLUSTRATIONS.

As the measurements in the illustrations have been made in metres, a scale of metres and English feet is given, showing their proportional values.

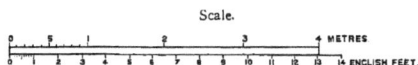

Scale.

NOTE.—For Sections of the Country and other descriptions of places mentioned in this work, *see* 'Across the Jordan,' by the same author.

THE JAULÂN.

THE Jaulân and Gaulanitis are names for one and the same tract of country in the middle of the now Turkish province of Syria. In the west, bordered by the Jordan fissure, it forms at the same time a part of the so-called East Jordan land, or Eastern Palestine. The Old Testament speaks of a place in Bashan, in the jurisdiction of the Manasseh tribe, called Golan (Deut. iv. 43), which in Joshua xx. 8, is mentioned as a free city, and in 1 Chron. vi. 71, as a Levite city. This probably answers to the present Sahem ej-Jaulân in Western Haurân.* Josephus (1 Wars, iv. 4) calls the place Golan, and the surrounding country Gaulanitis.

After the death of Herod the Great it must have been given over to the Tetrarch Philip, and was at

* Comp. Schumacher, 'Across the Jordan,' p. 91.

B

this time in its most flourishing period : a large
number of towns covered the middle and northern
part of the western slope, which, though stony, was
well watered and rich in pasture land. Some of
these, as Seleucia, Sogane, and Gamala, were turned
into fortifications according to Josephus (2 Wars,
xx. 6). The discovery of various extensive ruins,
which preserve their Roman names at the present
day, place the former prosperity of these towns
beyond doubt.

The remains of many of these old ruins, as will be
seen by the following description, are of undoubted
Jewish character ; and their architectural characteristics prove that the Jewish capability could make
itself freely felt even near Roman superiority.

During the Byzantine dominion over Gaulanitis,
Harit V. el-'Araj (530-572), called by the Romans
Aretas, and the most distinguished of the Ghassa-
nidic Phylarchs, was placed by Justinian at the head
of all the Arabian tribes in the Byzantine jurisdiction,
which comprehended Haurân and Damascus, as well
as the bank of Jordan, and therefore the Jaulân and
the Belka.

Already earlier, under the predecessors of that
Prince, viz., 'Amr I. (248-263) I. (248-263), Jabala I.
(330-360), Ma'ura, the spouse of Harits II. (360-373),
the Christians had founded settlements in the East
Jordan land, and especially monasteries, which at that

time were more frequently established in what is now called the Haurân than in the Jaulân. But owing to the invasion of Syria by the Persian king, Chosroes II., in 616, Christianity suffered a relapse, and this, coupled with the sect-hatred and party feeling of the Patriarchs of Constantinople, prepared the ground for the new teaching and sovereignty of Islam. The probably Persian name, Telestan, applied to the northern part of the country, is a memorial of the conquest of the Jaulân by Chosroes.

After the sanguinary defeat of the Byzantines at the River Yarmuk (634), in the southern extremity of the Jaulân, this land, with the whole of Syria, fell into the hands of the Arabs, who, however, have only per-petuated themselves here by monuments of mean architecture, although they may have kept the country itself at its highest state of existing culture. Never-theless, internal dissensions amongst the Moslem rulers added to the perpetual changes of succession, produced a retarding influence on the quiet progress of develop-ment, and when the armies of the Crusaders entered Syria they found a country whose decay had already commenced.

In Baldwin II.'s reign (1118), the sway of the Cross was again extended over the Jaulân. Whether the numberless crosses and Christian emblems which are found upon the ruins of the Jaulân date from the time of the Frankish rule, or that of the earlier Christian

B 2

period, is difficult to determine ; they may probably
be ascribed partly to one and partly to the other, as
they appear in Nu'aran, one of the cities mentioned
in the history of the Crusades ('Ritter, Erdk.' xvi.
p. 169), and also in proximity to el-Ahmediyeh, near
the name Ioxctin (Justinian ?). From the decline of
the Christian sovereignty in the Jaulân, and its recon-
quest by the Moslems, down to modern times, there is
little to relate.

Through invasions of the Mamelukes and Mongo-
lians in Syria the country seems to have sunk lower
and lower, and to have become in time the favourite
resting-place of the nomadic Bedawîn tribes, who had
no interest in the preservation of buildings, or the
guarding of firmly established abodes, whilst in the
plundering and subjection of the few remaining
settlements they found their pleasure and advantage.
In the year 1518 the Osman Sultan Selim I. took
Syria, and therewith also the Jaulân, from the Mamelukes, and bound it to the Turkish kingdom, to which
it has belonged till the present day.

The name of the country has never been altered in
all its changes of rule and circumstance, and the individual sounds remained the same, only the pronunciation of the first consonant (g) has softened in the
usual way, and the diphthong of the first syllable
(au) is in the vulgar tongue of to-day, as formerly in
the Old Testament, contracted into (o).

The following description mainly refers to the tract of land which is identical with the ancient Gaulanitis. Its boundaries are for the most part so clearly defined by nature that they have nearly always remained the same, with the exception that in the east the present demarcation is scarcely the old one, because on this side it was constantly altering according to the judgment of the existing Mutasarrif or Governor of the Haurân, and was sometimes removed further back, and again sometimes more forward, into the wide high plateau. As the surveyed map was to serve also as a plan for railway communication between 'Akka and Haifa, the sea-coast towns of Haurân and Damascus, it had the approval of the Vali, or Governor-General of Syria. So that to its author was granted the assistance of the officials belonging to the Liva of Haurân and the Kada el-Kuneitrah. He was consequently able to compare their opinion upon the orthography of the names of places with those collected in the places themselves, as well as to fix the boundaries of the district according to the testimony of the revenue officers.

The triangulation of the most important points was made by means of a theodolite. In the ground survey a water-level was used, and a Koniograph prepared by Herr D. O. Kersten, and very kindly left by him for this purpose, for which important service I must render this gentleman my best thanks.

The heights were obtained by an adjusted aneroid barometer, whilst the sea-level of the Lake of Tiberias —682·5 was considered the basis of my calculations. The divisions into degrees of length and breadth, as well as the triangulation, were finally executed and joined on to the large Map of the English Palestine Exploration Fund (Map of Western Palestine), for which triangulation I had plenty of material at my command. The scale of the map is that of the English map, viz., 'one inch to a mile.'*

The examination of the ruins could only be done disjointedly, according as the object of the work above pointed out permitted. I cannot, therefore, unconditionally guarantee an uninterrupted complete-ness in the description of the ruined places with which the Jaulân is simply swarming, for in addition to this the great distrust exhibited by the natives against travellers increases the difficulties of the examination of the land. The natives from fear of new taxes took care to conceal almost everything, so that information and guides could only be reached by threats of prison, and, as a rule, the discovering of ruins had to depend entirely upon myself.

A further difficulty consists in establishing the orthography of the names, for only very few of the Bedawin are acquainted with writing, and this always

* To accompany this work it has been reduced to the scale of ⅜ of an inch to a mile.

in so imperfect a manner that one comes upon glaring mistakes at every enquiry. The only thing that remained to me—most of the official books at these ruined places being missing—was to put frequently the same questions bearing on this to the different tribes, and to settle the orthography from their answer.

Guides acquainted with the language who hang about in the towns, Tiberias and Safed for instance, I hold as having very little weight as authorities on the orthographical correctness of the names, for it is exactly these persons who, from ignorance of the country and grammar, and above all 'pour vous faire plaisir,' make assertions which by observation at the places themselves are proved incorrect. The Khâtib, or scribe of a village, is still often, in spite of his simplicity, the most trustworthy source of help.

I was also careful, in drawing up the list of names of the places, to rigidly adhere to the original nomenclature, and not to be led into error by attempts at etymology.

Owing to the swampy river prevailing there in summer time, the Huleh marshes were not visited ; therefore the already-mentioned Sogana, presumably on the west of Jaulân (Josephus, 4 Wars, i, 1), is not marked on the map. Also the small northern end of the Sharah of Jaulân, near Baniâs, which includes a part of the southern slope of Hermon, had

to remain unexamined. It may be here remarked that
the ez Zawiyeh esh-Shurkîyeh of south-east Jaulân, a
district inclosed by the Yarmûk, Rukkâd and 'Allân
rivers, with also the neighbouring country to the east,
has been already set down by me on a map, and published by the English Palestine Exploration Fund,
on the scale of ⅜ of an inch to a mile, in the book,
' Across the Jordan,' 1886. At my first and more super-
ficial journey through the Jaulân and the Haurân, in
December, 1883, the Nahr er-Rukkâd was pointed out
to me as the boundary between the Jaulân and the
Haurân ; and I consequently agreed that the survey
of the Jaulân should extend to Nahr er-Rukkâd in
the east. Later, however, it transpired that the Nahr
el-'Allân was regarded as the boundary line between
the two districts. As a result of this mistake, the
following report and illustrating map do not include
the whole of the Jaulân. Nevertheless, recently the
place Sahem ej-Jaulân, which in 1884 was in the
administrative jurisdiction of the Jaulân, has again
been handed over to the Haurân seat of government in
Sheikh Sa'ad. Thus the extent and jurisdiction of the
one district of Haurân is still not definitely settled.

As to the orography of north Jaulân, I shall limit
myself to observations made on my first journey ; for
this district formed the basis of the researches of my
honoured friend and co-traveller, Herr Dr. Fritz
Noeblung, in the year 1885, and will be given in

detail in his geological description. With reference
to the historical dates obtained by individual information at the places visited, in the absence of other
literary testimony, I had to content myself with the
use of the following works :—

Josephus, in the English Translation of William
Whiston (Oxford, 1839); Ritter's 'Erdkunde,' vol.
xv., which contains an abstract of the important
journeys of Burckhardt and Seetzen ; Gustav. Flugel's
' History of the Arabians' (Leipzig, 1864), and
Baedeker's 'Palestine and Syria' (1875). I leave the
reader to draw from the collected material of descriptions, &c., further conclusions upon the historic past
of the places treated here.

B.—POSITION, EXTENT, LIMITS, AND ADMINISTRA-
TION OF THE JAULÂN.

The entire area of modern Jaulân, including ez
Zawîyeh esh-Shurkîyeh and Sha'rah in the north, is
about 560 square miles. By the Jaulân is meant only
the high plateau and a part of its declivity, viz., the
north-west portion sloping from the Huleh marshes :
and bounded in the west by Jordan, south-west by the
Lake of Tiberias, north by the declivities of Hermon
and the Wâdy el-Adjam, north-east by Jedur or Nahr
er-Rukkâd, and east and south by Haurân or the
Nahr el-Allân, and in the south by 'Ajlûn or the

River Yarmuk. Politically, the Jaulân forms one of
the administrative districts (Kaimakâmîyeh) of the
Sanjak or the Liva of Haurân (with the seat of
government of a Kaimakam in el-Kuneitrah), and
as such is under the Mutasarrif of the Haurân at
Sheikh Sa'ad.

The Jaulân itself is divided into four districts : (1)
Mu diriyeh esh-Sharah (in the north), chief town and
residence of the Mudir is Mejdel esh-Shems ; (2) el-
Kuneitrah (in the centre), chief town and residence of
the Kaimakâmîyeh is el-Kuneitrah ; (3) ez Zawîyeh
el-Ghurbiyeh (south), chief town and residence of the
Mukhtar is Kefr el-Ma ; (4) ez-Zawîyeh esh-Shurkîyeh,
(east), chief town and residence of a Mukhtar is esh-
Shejarah.

The Mudir and Mukhtar are inferior officials of the
Kaimakam. The Mukhtars, properly only village
magistrates, have to look after the punctual payment
of the taxes, and are responsible for them. They
receive no salary, and must even support the government officers whilst on their expeditions ; but they
are at the same time exempt from taxation, and may
present an account in el-Kuneitrah for the fodder
consumed by the horses of the gen-d'armes, which is
discharged according to the letter of the law. The
heads of the chief families of the country, the village
sheikhs of Fîk, Skufîyeh, Kefr el-Ma, el-'Al, Khisfin,
and esh-Shejarah, form an administrative council ;

these, with occasionally a representative of the Jerkessen and Bedawîn tribes, compose a council side
by side with the government official. The first are,
however, usually represented by the village Sheikh
Kefr el-Ma, who therefore counts for the fourth
member of the proper Mejlis el-Idara (conseil ad-
ministratif). The Mudir of Mejdel esh-Shems ought
properly to be an independent official ; for the most
part he receives his instructions from el-Kuneitrah.
Meanwhile a plan appears to have been projected to
separate this Mudîrîyeh from Jaulân, and to assign it
to Merj 'Ayûn.

The entire armed force of Kada el-Kuneitrah consists of from fifteen to twenty mounted gen-d'armes
(Khaiyal el-Mîreh), an officer and a police soldier :
which is quite enough in times of peace to settle the
small feuds between the tribes, and maintain authority
of the government.

C.—THE NATURE OF THE GROUND, PLANTS AND ANIMALS, IRRIGATION AND CLIMATE, OF THE JAULÂN.

According to the nature of the soil, the Jaulân may
be divided into two districts : (1) stony in the northern
and middle part, (2) smooth in the south and more
cultivated part. Both divisions form a part of the
great high plateau, which, in the widest sense, is

known as Haurân : and which extends from Hermon
and Damascus on the south to the Steppe Hamâd
and 'Ajlûn, eastward to the Syrian Desert and Jebel
el-Drûz, and westward to the Jordan.

The plateau of the Jaulân, commencing at a height
of 974 feet in the south (Shâfât Mobarah), gradually
reaches a height of more than 3,625 feet in the north
(Merj el-Buk'âti), independently of the volcanic
mountains, which reach a height of 4,244 feet, and
has therefore an average height of 2,950 feet above
the level of the Mediterranean Sea, or 3,632 feet above
the Lake of Tiberias.

In its diagonal direction the land makes a quick
(and as a consequence of the lava stream) terrace-like
ascent from the western Jordan slope, from an average
height of 1,640 feet in the east to a watershed of
3,000 feet in between the foot of the Tell Abu en-
Nedâ and the Hami-Kursu. It then slopes towards
the bed of the Nahr er-Rukkâd, and again ascends
east of this latter towards Haurân. The highest point
of the plateau lies in the north, whilst in the south-
west corner of ez Zawiyeh el-Ghurbîyeh, consequently at the further extremity of Jaulân, the lowest
part is found.

Taking Shârah and Ghôr into consideration, there
is a matter of the significant difference in height of +
4,460 feet (about Mejdel esh-Shems), and − 656 feet
(Ghôr at ed-Duer), that is a difference of 5,116 feet.

Stony Jaulân (esh-Shàrah, el-Kuneitrah and the upper part of ez Zawîyeh esh-Shurkîyeh) is an altogether rough and wild country, covered with masses of lava which are poured out from the countless volcanoes and spread in every direction. Although of little use agriculturally, it is all the more valuable as pasturage for the numerous herds of the Bedawîn, and serves as the ideal of such a 'land of spring pasturage,' Belâd er-Rabi. Wherever between the hard solid basaltic blocks there is a spot of earth, or an opened rift visible, the most luxurious grass springs up both in winter and spring time, and affords the richest green fodder for the cattle of the Bedawîn ; for this part of the Jaulân possesses a great source of wealth in its perennial springs, so that the heat of summer never scorches all the vegetation, and round the springs there is always a fringe of green. A man travelling through the country at two different periods of the year, say about August or September, and then in February or March, would scarcely recognise it. In summer, bare masses of stone block up the road and hem the traveller in at every step, and the country is of a monotonous dismal character ; whilst in the spring the former, as well as the heaps of ruins, are overgrown with grass to the height of a man. Then the myrtles and oak bushes are no longer alone in springing out from the lava blocks; the ruins have disappeared, the land is clothed

in verdure, and it is only the stumbling of the beasts
on the impassable road, the ascent of ever fresh blocks
of rock, and a glance at the characteristic conical-
shaped rows of volcanoes, which brings to the traveller
the conviction that he is treading the same Jaulân
under a different aspect. As a consequence of the
efflorescent volcanic lava and deposited ashes the soil
is very productive, and besides grass, wheat, and
barley, peas (Hummus), lentils, beans, camel fodder
(Kursanneh), white maize and yellow maize flourish.
There is thus a large space which is comparatively
stoneless ; for instance, the plateau near the watershed,
which is bounded by the mountains Tell el-Baram,
Tell el-Urâm, Tell Abu en-Nedâ, Tell Abu Yusef, the
spurs of the Hami Kursu and the Tellul el-Mukhfy,
and which is tended and cultivated by the Jerkessen.
Even the crater of the mighty Tell Abu en-Nedâ is
cultivated, and said to bear most valuable produce.

Recently, in the lowlands of the Huleh lake, where
there is no lack of water, rice has been sown, the
quality of which leaves nothing to be desired, and
which forms a more lucrative article of commerce
than grain—the Haurân soil appearing to have been
made for its successful cultivation. The yellow,
so called European maize (dura franje, or safra), is
again sown in the latter part of summer on the well-
watered places of the plateau, and thus the land
yields a double crop. An excellent quality of

tobacco flourishes in the north country near Za'ôra ;
it is concealed in beds of manure so as to elude
detection by the officers, and as soon as the leaves
wither the inveterate Bedawîn smokers use it un-
prepared.

A few years back stony Jaulân must have been
covered with a thick growth of forest trees. This
is proved by the names Sháfât es-Sindianeh, 'oak
top,' and the designation formerly given to the
volcanoes Tellul el-Hish,* 'an ambush'; the still
extensive oak woods at the foot of Tell Abu en-
Nedâ and Tell Abu el-Khanzír, the thick oak underwood of the declivities of Tell el-Ahmar, Hami
Kursu, Sháfât es-Sindianeh, and the beautiful oak
trees which singly and in groups cover the low
plateau in the north of the Batihah. Throughout
the north the evergreen oak is of the Sindian (stone
oak) kind, with small prickly leaves and little acorns.
The Mallul kind is rarer. Whilst in the north of the
Batihah there is a kind of winter oak (Quercus
ægilops) to be found with a thick rough bark and
smooth large oak-apples in wide shallow cups. Of
other trees we find the evergreen Butmeh (Pistavia
terebinthia), which is widely distributed. These are
mostly found in the vicinity of the oaks, but are

* Burckhardt has made this name known under the form of
"Hersch." (Comp. 'Burckhardt's Journey,' i. 438. J. G. Wetzstein, d. Batanäischi Giebelgebirge, 1884, 10 f.)

easily distinguished by their most beautiful growth
and better and stronger shade. A single butm is
often found alone in the midst of fields shading the
grave of some holy Moslem. It then receives the
surname Fakîreh ('poor'), is thereby safe from all
outrage, and can attain unmolested a great age. No
Moslem would dare to break off a branch or even
remove a withered twig, for the saying goes that such
a deed would bring upon it heavy divine punishment.

In proof, the Bedawîn Fellahîn relate with alacrity
many examples to the traveller, as for instance, one
man, after some outrage on the Fakîreh, broke his
arm ; or the donkey, carrying the sacred burden, fell
down dead ; or the room in which the wood was
stored fell in and injured the possessor ; in fact, never
once was a branch bent down but it called up the
judgment of the divine wrath. Once, when a Fakîreh
standing in a village obstructed my inspection, I
asked my guide either to break off or bend down one
of the branches ; but neither requests nor threats
availed, and on undertaking the matter myself I saw
the simple-minded Fellahîn regarding me with horror
and awaiting the fate that was to overtake me. A
similar deed is, however, not to be recommended to
a traveller, unless he is furnished with good recommendations from the Government. Another kind of
lore is the Zârûra, or white thorn, which, however,
like the myrtle growing on the slopes of the Wâdy

Dabûra, is rarer. Along the watercourses, and
without exception in the ravines of the wâdies conveying water, we find the perpetually blooming rose-
coloured oleander (Difleh), the wild fig (Tineh), and
less frequently the tamarisk (tarfa), the plane tree
(dulba), the carob bean tree (kharrub), and the wild
vine (dalieh pl. dawâll). Reeds, Kasab or Kuseb,
often entirely clothe slopes where there are small
gushing springs. On the western slope of central
Jaulân (Dabûra) liquorice (?) (Umm es-Sûs) root is
found very plentifully. Stony Jaulân, as indeed the
entire plateau, has very few fruit trees. One scarcely
sees, even in the villages, a Rummaneh (pomegranate bush) or a fig tree ; Za'ôra, and 'Aîn Fit are
exceptional. The Circassians are also beginning to
cultivate trees, although they greatly prefer the
cultivation of pasture-land ; but still every now and
again in el-Kuneitrah one finds trees bearing fruit.
On the other hand, these same Circassians are
rapidly lessening the oak woods, as they cut down the
fine trunks and carry them on their horrible squeak-
ing two-wheeled carts, drawn by oxen, to sell as
timber. One such I recently met in South Haurân,
where for centuries no cart can possibly have
traversed the stoneless ground.

An attempt at vine cultivation was recently made
by the Emir of 'Arab el-Fadel in the neighbourhood of Skêk, but his kinsmen apparently preferred

c

resting under a shady pavilion to the work of the
vineyard.

The slopes of the plateaus towards the Jordan and
the Lake of Huleh are tolerably steep, and as their
tops are crowned by rugged blocks of lava, which
decompose piece-meal and roll down below, the last
part of the ascent is most difficult.

The wâdies resemble narrow, and often frightfully
deep, chasms, and into their yawning depths rush
seaward flowing streams. One of the deepest and
steepest of these channels is the Wâdy el-Yehûdîyeh,
near the ruin of the same name. The walls, which
are basaltic in the upper division, and composed of
limestone in the lower, are perpendicular, often
indeed overhanging, and with a width of 656 feet in
the upper part of the wâdy, attain a height of not
less than 492 feet.

What finally distinguishes stony Jaulân from the
southern, and also the Haurân plateau, is the large
number of extinguished volcanoes.

One group of these is found in the east, near the
Rukkâd, with the rocky el-Kulei'âh crater as the
most southern point, and ending in the north with
the Hâmi Kursu, the lava of which reaches el-
Kuneitrah.

The most marked and well known of their summits
is Tell el-Fâras, 3,110 feet high, whilst the Hami
Kursu reaches a height of 3,930 feet. Tellul el-Humr

and Tellul el-Asbah lie somewhat east. A second group extends almost as a continuation of the first in a north-west-northerly direction from el-Kuneitrah to the Birket er-Râm. At first a low hill range, they reach, at Tell esh-Sheikhah, a height of 4,245 feet. There is a third group, which joins the second one in the north, surrounds Merj el-Buk'âti, and runs parallel to the first in a southerly direction to Tell Abu Yûsef. 3,375 feet, making this the most southerly spur. The largest and most interesting peak of this group is Tell Abu en-Nedâ, with a maximum height of 4,124 feet ; very well marked, though subordinate, is the Tell el-Urâm, 4,042 feet. Further, the small Tell el-Baram, 3,720 feet, and the peak Tell el-Ahmar in the north, 4,060 feet, whose lava stream reaches the slopes of the marshes of Huleh.

In the south, somewhat westward, the double-peaked Tell Abu el-Khanzîr, 3,819 feet, rises. Besides these high and extraordinary cone-shaped craters, there are the low hills of er-Rumsaniyeh, Tell el-Talâyà, Umm ed-Danânîr, and Tell el-Ferj. These follow the extended course of the third group towards the south, and finally the Tell Jôkhadar ends them. This latter is equally distant south with el-Kulei'âh, but 2 miles more west from the chain of volcanic groups, which includes a length of 20 miles by a breadth of 2 miles. In earlier descriptions of travels these mountains of

north Jaulân are distinguished by the general name
of 'Tellul el-Hesh,' or 'el-Hish,' but careful inquiry
on this point proves that if this name has not entirely
disappeared from the memory of the people, it is
very rarely known.   I have, therefore, not written
this name on the map.   Although these volcanoes
ought to be carefully considered in a detailed account
of the places and names of Jaulân, I shall nevertheless refer again, readers, so far as their geological
connection with upper Jaulân is concerned, to the
detailed geological examination by my travelling
companion, Dr. Noeblung, to which I have appended
my testimony concerning the craters of Tell el-Fâras
and Tell Abu en-Nedâ.

South Jaulân—that is, ez Zawîyeh el-Ghurbîyeh
—is, in opposition to North Jaulân, from Khisfin
onward, stoneless.   The lava-rock surface gradually
disappears, and in its place is a rich dark-brown lava
soil, which is prevalent in the whole of the Haurân,
and the fertility of which cannot be too highly praised.
Grain—i.e., wheat and barley—flourish here in large
quantities, and with Turkish maize (dura) and
Simsim are almost the exclusive cultivations.   On
the other hand, there is less pasture-land in the level
plains of ez Zawîyeh el-Ghurbîyeh, and the grass
withers very quickly in summer.   As perennial
springs are lacking in the high plateau, the villages
are mostly built on the edge of the plateau, where

abundant springs are to be found to this day. Instead of the tent Bedawîn of the north-west stony Jaulân, we find in the Zawîyeh colonized peasants, who have established large villages and cultivated the ground as much as their primitive agricultural implements permit. Much good land, therefore, lies fallow, for the Fellahîn only cultivate an area round their village which is not too large for them to reach and cultivate in a day. How many thousands of acres are languishing for rational cultivation, and how easy it would be in this wide, healthy, high plateau of Jaulân and Haurân, to develop a settled industry which would yield valuable results !

The culture on the high plateau of South Jaulân is nearly extinct. The eye seeks in vain for a shady branch, although it may occasionally happen that one's wish is gratified by a terebinth (butm) hung with gay-coloured rags, which have been devoted to the Neby (Holy One) by distressed women and sick persons ; these, however, may be counted. On the slopes, however, and wherever the axe does not reach, there is a more flourishing plant growth.

The wide smooth Wâdy Masâûd show a really fine amount of oak trees, which reaches to the high plateau, bordered by the Yarmûk in the extreme south-west corner of Jaulân. The Kûlàt el-Husn is also covered with beautiful isolated oaks and tere-

binths (butm). The Wâdy es-Semakh grows, beside
some oaks and terebinths, a thorn-bush called Sidr,
and a stroll along the narrow east-coast strip of
Bahr et-Tûbarîya soon brings us to the Dom-bush,
which has thorns bent inwards, and which seems
peculiarly indigenous to the Jordan valley and the
land round the Lake of Tiberias.   There is a distinc-
tion between two kinds of these Dom-bushes, viz.,
Dom-sidr and Dom-rubet (? red) ;   both have small
light-green thin leaves similar to the terebinthus
foliage, and bear a delicious hawberry kind of sweet
fruit, which are eaten with appreciation by the
Bedawîn, and also gathered and sold in the cities.
In the upper Jordan valley the Dom-bush seldom
attains a greater height than 13 feet, and never
ceases being green, blooming, and fruitful, so that the
traveller in the hot Jordan valley has at least one
enjoyment.   Although it is the only shade-affording
plant of the upper Jordan valley, a man only avails
himself of its shelter from necessity, for the slightest
breath of wind brings the malicious thorns in contact,
which, in spite of the greatest caution, manage to
bury themselves in the dress and skin of the rester.
The wood is white, and extraordinarily hard and
tough.

   In fruit trees, also, the ez Zawîyeh is poor ;   it is only
in the village and Wâdy Fîk, and in the tributary,
Wâdy Abûd, that we find beautiful olive groves.

These are cultivated by the inhabitants of Fîk, and produce a good yearly crop, which supplies the surrounding country with olive-oil, so rarely met with in Haurân.

On the western declivities of ez Zawîyeh, towards the sea, Kharrub and Abhar bushes (lilac, Styrax officinalis, according to the 'Memoirs' of the Palestine Exploration Fund) grow singly; and in the Yarmûk and Rukkâd valley are oleanders, plane trees, wild grapes, and canes. The villages have some pomegranates and fig trees.

In spite of this absence of wood growth in the southern high plateau, it may be assumed from tradition, and the names still existing, as Sirb el-Butm, Sirbit el-Khararib (Terebinthus and Kharrub woods), Enjum el-Butm, Enjum el-Abhar (Hill of Terebinthus, Hill of Lilac), from the single old trees still extant, that the wood growth of the high plateau was at one time in a better condition. The climate and soil are no hindrance to increased growth of the trees; but the natives, with the aim of being comfortably warm in winter, cut down everything they can reach, without an idea of substitution. The wood-saints of the villages sufficiently prove that fuel is considered a treasured article on the plateau. For the absolute security of the stock of wood laboriously collected during the summer months, it is stored as near as possible to one of the holy graves by

the Mujjenneh, Wely, or Makam, which are present
in every village ; no one dares then, with the exception of the foreign traveller's cook, to lay a trespassing
hand on the treasure. It is more secure there than
in the owner's hut ; and for the same reason agricultural implements are deposited near to the Neby.

The declivities of southern Jaulân to Lake
Tiberias and the Yarmûk, or Sheriât el-Menâdireh,
are throughout steep in the upper part. The high
plateau is sharply edged by a layer of 'Hummus,'
covered with fragments of lava. Great blocks dis-
integrate from the upper layer and roll into the
valley, or mass themselves on the third division of
the terrace-shaped declivities. The middle portion of
the slopes is less steep ; it consists of the sloping
heaps from the upper terrace, and has gradually
spread itself out to a 'Hummus' layer which has
been shot down from the high plateau. Mountain
slips are not unfrequent. Finally, the lowest portion,
viz., down to the Sea of Tiberias, is composed of a
multitude of rubbish cones, with little water channels
in between—a formation caused by the loosened
masses of mountains from above. In the Yarmûk
valley, instead of cone-heaps, are basaltic walls
98 feet broad, bordering the river ; but here, too, the
terrace formation is clearly visible.

The declivities in the Batihah are smoother to
ascend and less steep.

The most important animals in the Jaulân are soon disposed of. Besides the jackal (Wâwch) and the hyena, a wolf with grey fur is to be met with. I met such a one in December, 1883, in the neighbourhood of Kefr el-Ma, probably come down from Hermon. In the ruined places especially are a plentiful number of Syrian foxes, called Abu Ahseineh, with their reddish-brown tails and light-brown fur ; without the tail they measure 23 inches, but are only from 15 to 18 inches high. Likewise among the ruins are to be found numerous small grey wild cats, whose fury, directly they are wounded, is well known to the inhabitants, one raises unwillingly, although it is not unseldom exhibited. Gazelles are constantly to be seen in herds of 4 to 20 quietly resting. A kind of stag with large horns is supposed to make its appearance sometimes, but I never caught sight of one. Wild boars live in large numbers in the neighbourhood and thickets of el-Hammeh and el-Mukhaibeh, on the Yarmûk, also in the deeply indented woods.

The Jaulân is poorly furnished with bright-coloured birds. Besides the thistle finch and common finch, there is the field lark and sparrow, which here, as everywhere else, carries on its thieving existence. In spring large swarms of wild doves (Rukti) and starlings (Zarzur) injure the seeds. Large coveys of partridges (Hâjal) are to be met with in sheltered

bushy places. As to dangerous reptiles in stony
Jaulân, a light-brown viper, about 3 feet in length, is
found ; it has a thick head, thick body, and short
tail, and herds of these do great damage. In the
little water-basin found in the wâdies in summer, and
also in the small running brooks, there are innumer-
able poisonous water-snakes of a dark colour (ash
grey), and measuring 3 feet to 4½ feet in length. The
entwined and partly water-growing roots of the
oleander bushes make a favourite hiding-place for
them, from which they dart out upon their prey. The
inhabitants are frightened of these water-snakes, and
avoid bathing in such water channels. I have con-
vinced myself of the harmlessness of a black-spotted,
dark, large snake (probably belonging to the family
Colubridar, named Zamens—see ' Botiger Rephtien
und Amphibien von Syrien,' 1880), which is frequently met with in Western Palestine. This, as,
indeed, every other snake, is regarded by the natives
as poisonous.

There are quantities of tarantulas and scorpions to
be found on the east bank of the Lake of Tiberias ;
the pitching of a tent there, as I know from my
own experience, may have grievous consequences.

To get a clear impression of the irrigation of the
Jaulân one must always bear in mind that the
highest point of the longitudinal profile is in the
north, whilst the deepest of the same is in the south-

west, and the transverse profile of the north and central Jaulân falls into two sides, right and left, towards the Jordan and Rukkâd.

From the water-shed, which, as we have seen, reaches a height of about 3,000 feet between the two extended groups of volcanoes, spring many small watercourses.

Flowing thence at first only as perennial springs over the surface of the ground, they soon cut deeper and deeper clefts in the same ; and about the district between el-'Aselîyeh, Kubbet ed-Dhahr, el-Kusbiyeh, Washarah, and el-Kubbeh, where the plateau makes an abrupt descent, they reach a depth of 492 feet and more below the neighbouring country—these water-channels, or wâdies, conveying only an insignificant amount of water in summer ; but in winter they swell so suddenly as to hinder traffic and form giant mountain streams, with cataracts bringing down and depositing at their mouths a mass of boulders. The course of these wild streams divides in two directions south from Tell Abu el-Khanzîr and west from the volcanic group of Tell Abu en-Nedâ. The first, and certainly the most important group, embrace those which originate in greater or less proximity to the southerly foot of the Tell Abu el-Khanzîr and Tell Abu Yusef, make, after numerous windings, a south-westerly course and then unite to three powerful mountain streams, which, under the names of Wâdy es-Safâ, ed-Dalieh, and es-Senâm,

enter the plain el-Batihah. There, during summer,
they lose their water either wholly or partly, so that
the course of these wâdies to the Sea of Tiberias is
only recognisable by the stratum of material which the
water has brought along with it. During summer the
Wâdy ed-Dalich, on the border of Batihah, evaporates,
and the Wâdy es-Senâm is completely dried up ; the
Wâdy es-Safâ alone in the hot weather has water.
The course of this wâdy is not, counting windings, on
the whole 16 miles in length ; and there is a difference
of 3,116 feet in height between the source and where
it enters the Sea of Galilee.

The wild streams of the second group rise along the
western slopes of Tell Abu el-Khanzîr, Abu en-Nedâ,
and barren Tell el-Ahmar runs parallel towards
west-south-west and west, and discharge themselves
into the marshes and Lake of Huleh. Only a few
small disappearing wâdies rise 'upon the slopes themselves, and make quick short courses to the Jordan.
The streams also belonging to the second group can
hardly be regarded as perennial.

They all dry up with the exception of Wâdy Dabura
and Wâdy el-Hamd, where even in late summer a little
water always sparkles down. During rainy season
they increase less than the ones belonging to the first
group, for their course is considerably shorter, amounting at best to no more than $7\frac{1}{2}$ miles. The difference
in height between the source and the mouth amounts

at its highest to 2,952 feet (W. Dabura), and to 1,640 feet at its lowest, in an extent of 2½ miles to 3½ miles. The wâdy of both groups do not sink gradually to this remarkable depth, but fall for the most part in terraces.

East of the volcanoes and the water-shed of northern Jaulân, that is towards the low lands of Rukkâd, there are no water channels worthy of mention ; they are only perennial and sporadic springs, whose short course, even in the rainy season, has only a bed of a few metres deep, which is owing to the slight difference of height in their course. The water channels of central Jaulân rise on the southern edge of the watershed, at the place where it makes a steep incline between the southern outlets of the volcanic chain, and soon make for the west, towards the Lake of Tiberias. Before its mouth the Wâdy Joramâyeh enters Batihah and unites with the Wâdy es-Senâm. The water of these valleys flows at first slowly over the surface, which is already less stony, gradually grows into a swift torrent and tumbles from a great height over basaltic terraces. The most remarkable example of this kind is afforded by the Wâdy Bâzûk near a Tell of the same name, whose stream (according to a measure designed for the purpose), beginning with a depth of only 10 feet beneath the surface of the country, after a length of 656 feet falls down a height of 531 feet, in cataracts of 66 feet and 100 feet. The same thing occurs in

the Wâdy Joramâyeh. The Wâdy esh-Shukeiyif and
the double-branched more distant Wâdy es-Semakh
are less violent. The length of Wâdy Joramâyeh
reaches, at the most, 13 miles; the difference of
height between spring and lake being about 2,952
feet. These valleys of central Jaulân, in opposition to
the narrow cleft like one of north Jaulân, which are
only a few hundred feet in breadth, are two and more
miles broad ; they are quite charming towards the lake,
are in part built over and inhabited by Bedawîn, and
like Wâdy es-Semakh, for instance, covered with ruins.
Some water flows along the bottom, which only in
years of very abundant water reaches in summer the
lake-basin. Every such stream in the Jaulân is extraordinarily rich in fish. Finally, the wâdy of southern
Jaulân are more insignificant. The two most note-
worthy are: the pleasant woody Wâdy Masâûd, moist-
ened by a stream which discharges into the Yârmûk
in the south Jaulân, and which is 5½ miles long, not
counting windings, and which makes a fall of 1,508
feet, and Wâdy Fîk; this, which is very rocky in the
upper part, runs northward past Kŭlât el-Husn to the
lake, and is fed by a small stream.

The length of the wâdy scarcely amounts to 3½
miles, and its entire fall is about 1,800 feet. The
other wâdy are small side valleys of the Yârmûk and
Rukkâd.

Besides these small floods, which begin and end in

the Jaulân proper, we must mention those larger
channels which are outside the Jaulân, and either
stretch through it or in part form its boundaries.
There are (1) Nahr es-Sa'âr, in the north of Sharah;
(2) the Jordan, in part the western border of Jaulân;
(3) the Nahr er-Rukkâd, between Jaulân and Jedûr;
(4) Nahr el-'Allân, the east boundary of entire
Jaulân ; and finally (5) the two latter, which, joined,
form the largest river, the Shariat el-Menâdîreh,
Yarmûk, the southern boundary of Jaulân.

(1.) The Nahr es-Sa'âr, beginning on the southern
slopes of Hermon as a clear, fresh stream, flows in
a southerly direction towards Merj el Yafûreh, and
propels some mills on the east side of this valley,
then crosses the Merj in an even—often sluggish—
course, and joins at Birket er-Râm with a small confluent, the Seil el Yafûreh, which turns a mill near a
pond of the same name. At el-Mes'adi it falls over
rugged steps into a deep ravine, which, from there
onward, bears the name of Wâdy el-Hoshabah, and
divides esh Shârah into two parts. Wedged in by high
rock walls, it soon changes from its southerly direction
to north-west-north and enters the plateau at Baniâs,
uniting her with the Nahr Baniâs. The valley of
Wâdy el-Hoshabah widens in its upper part, and
then narrows lower down into terraces, leaving the
rushing brook only a very limited space. At Birket
er-Râm the Nahr es-Sa'âr is about 8 feet broad, but

scarcely a foot deep. In the vicinity of its source the water is clear, but in the Merj (plain) becomes a dirty-green colour, covered with swamp vegetation, which it loses first in its swifter course in Wâdy el-Hoshabah. The whole length reaches about 9 miles ; the total fall between the Merj and Baniâs is 2,362 feet.

(2.) The Jordan, or esh-Sherîâh.

The largest river in Palestine, has been sufficiently treated in the 'Memoirs' of the Palestine Exploration Fund and in other places, and is only of importance to us so far as it refers to the portion in the district between the Lake of Huleh and the Sea of Tiberias. Its slow course down to the Lake of Huleh is surrounded by marshes and papyrus woods ; when it emerges from this lake it has an uniform flow inasmuch as in a stretch of 10 miles it falls 689 feet. Thus, from $+$ 7 feet at the Lake of Huleh to $-$ 682 feet at the Lake of Tiberias.

The broad Huleh marshes narrow beneath the lake to a small valley, through which the stream glides down to the Batihah and into the Lake of Tiberias.

On account of the marsh fever, the Huleh marshes are in bad repute ; their miasma may be observed on the high-lying Mejdel esh-Shems.

The Jordan, also, between the above-mentioned lakes, produces this same fever, in consequence of the heated air wedged inside the high ridges of the valley. I know, from certainty, that a single night spent in late summer near Jisr Benât Yâkûb, is enough to impregnate the body with fever. The water of the river is muddy, in spite of its stony bed overlaid with rubble; oleanders, canes, willows, and other shrubs grow on its banks. At its discharge into Lake Tiberias it flows slowly, and is 147 feet broad, with a depth of 3 feet. However, this measure increases or lessens according to the time of the year.

(3.) The Nahr er-Rukkâd.*

This most important river of Jaulân has its source in the southern declivities of Hermon, in the western Wâdy el-'Ajam. It is from the spring 'Ain el-Beidah (3,394 feet), close to the boundary between el-Kuneitrah and Wâdy el'-Ajam, that the channel of the Rukkâd, otherwise dry, gets fed. Towards the north this latter is only a little sunk below the surface of the ground; but the whole country inclines towards it from the east, and during the melting of the snow and heavy downpours of rain, is highly flooded. It is for this reason that at Sueiseh the channel is spanned by an arched bridge (Jisr es-Sueiseh), which is fairly preserved. The small springs, which scarcely moisten the land between 'Ain el-Beidah and Ghadîr el-Bustân, are not worthy of mention. On the other hand, large springs appear at Ghadîr ej-Jamus and Ghadîr el-Bustân, so that the

* *See* 'Across the Jordan,' p. 13, Schumacher.

Rukkâd, from thence onward to the lower bridge,
Jisr er-Rukkâd, is never, even in summer, quite
dried up. The bridge road stands 1,610 feet above
the sea : that is, 1,784 feet lower than 'Ain el-Beidah.
The channel is from 16 feet to 19 feet below the
surrounding country, and is still some hundreds of
feet wide.

Scarcely 656 feet beyond Jisr er-Rukkâd the
natural features change ; here the water suddenly
dashes over perpendicular basaltic rocks 82 feet
high, and lower down are many other cascades.
The wide bed contracts to a narrow cleft, whose
perpendicular walls fall to a great depth. This
part of the Rukkâd, so an old Bedawîn told
me, was called by the Bedawîn tribes (Jarab Sakhar)
who formerly dwelt there, and who now camp
near Nazareth, and in the plain of Jezreel—Hami
Sakhar, that is, 'Protector of Sakhar'—indicating
that in a time of pursuit no food could follow
them here. This name is still known, as well as
that of Rukkâd, and is once mentioned thus by
Burckhardt ('Ritter Erdk.' xv., p. 356). After a
course of about 5 miles from its first fall the Rukkâd
receives from the east a fine stream—the Wâdy
Seisûn, whose water likewise falls down from the
plateau, and can be heard at a great distance. At
the same time, between Jamlch and Kefr el-Ma, the
ravine widens to a distance of 1¼ miles, and is divided

by the Râs el-Hâl (or Tell el-Ehdeb), one of the gliding mountains loosed from the overhanging bank itself, into two parts. The Rukkâd, therefore, between this and Kefr el-Ma, flows thither at a height of 538 feet above sea-level, and is joined further down by another little wâdy, whose source is between the Tell and Jamleh, and which descends from a greater height from the southern hanging coast bank. The long extended gliding hill of Râs el-Hâl, which has an almost perpendicular incline of fully 524 feet to the Rukkâd ; the narrow northern ravine, with its gloomy basaltic walls above, and white chalk walls in the river bed, and the foaming waterfall of Wâdy Seisûm, gives the country an extraordinary picturesque aspect. The valley widens still more, and the Rukkâd flows tolerably quick over large basaltic blocks to its union with the Yarmûk at Tell el-Ferdâweh (or Tell el-Hâweh), which lies 154 feet beneath the level of the Mediterranean Sea. In summer time, however, its water evaporates before it reaches this river. Its entire length, from 'Ain el-Beidah to Yarmûk, is 38 miles, the difference in altitude of the two points being 3,549 feet. In the bed of the river are a large number of boulders, which roll along the crumbling soft limestone, of which the bed of the river and a part of the slope consists, with a swiftly-destroying effect. In spring time, and when the snow of the high mountains of the Jaulân and Hermon melts, these boulders are set in motion

by huge masses of water and obstruct all traffic.
A proof of the great size of these floods is shown
by the heap deposited on the side of the river
basin beneath the Râs el-Hâl, the breadth of which
is 300 to 400 feet. The Rukkâd swarms with savoury
fish, especially carp, which are easily caught with
nets. The banks of the lower half are luxuriant with
oleanders, wild figs, plane trees, canes, also wild
grapes and willows. With the exception of the above
mentioned Wâdy Seisûn, the Rukkâd has no confluent of any importance. The Wâdy Ser'âi, Sîhân,
and Hetâl, as well as a large number of springs upon
the declivities of Zâwîyeh el-Ghurbîyeh certainly
hold water constantly, but these soon evaporate in
the deeply-notched valley. The Seil el-Ghôr, which
flows into the Rukkâd at Kefr el-Ma, conveys plenty
of water to this latter during the rainy season.

(4.) The Nahr el-'Allân.*—This frontier river between the Jaulân and the Haurân, which with the
Rukkâd and Yarmûk surrounds ez Zawîyeh esh-
Shurkîyeh of the Jaulân, proceeds from the high
plateau of Jedur, and makes a less divergent southerly
course than the Rukkâd, beneath the village of el-
Ekseir, and about 56 feet above (east) the Rukkâd
flows into the Yarmûk. Although its channel is
shorter than that of the Rukkâd, it bears a great
resemblance to this latter.

* *See* 'Across the Jordan,' p. 16, Schumacher.

Instead of a moderate fall at the beginning, numerous cataracts between high basaltic walls suddenly appear enclosing the narrow ravine. They only convey a little water in summer time, and first begin to get fuller in the spring.

The most important river of the east Jordan land, and at the same time the most powerful tributary of the Jordan, is the (5) Yarmûk or Sherî'at el-Menâdireh. It was called Hieromax by the Greeks and Romans, whilst in more recent time, in consequence of the Bedawîn tribe 'Arab el-Menâdireh camping on its valleys, and cultivating its slopes, it received the name of Sherî'at (watering place for animals) el-Menâdireh. It, too, rises as an abundant stream in north Jedur at the northern edge of Haurân, pursues a long southerly course to Tell el-Ashâry in Haurân, and then strikes a decided westerly direction till it joins the Nahr el-'Allân, not far from the village of Heit in Haurân. Its name up to here is called Wâdy el-Ehreir, also its old designation of Irak or ('Arak) is still known. United with the 'Allân it flows for some miles south-west, and then unites with Wâdy Zeizûm and Wâdy esh-Shelaleh, both plenteous rivers descending from Haurân. From here onwards it bears the name Sherî'at el-Menâdireh, and at Tell el-Ferdâweh, at the side of Wâdy Keleit, absorbs the Rukkâd. It then flows swiftly with a rapid current in a south-westerly direction till it reaches the Ghôr, past el-Mukhaibeh and el-Hammeh. It approaches the Jordan in a more southerly direction, to which, near the old Mejâmiá bridge, at least it conveys as much water as the former itself contains.

As to other tributaries of the Yarmûk, entirely disregarding a number of smaller springs, I will mention further the Wâdies el-Ku'elby and Samar, or 'Ain el-Ghazâleh of 'Ajlun, the Wâdy ez-Zeyyatîn of western Haurân, and the earlier mentioned Wâdy Masâûd of south-western Jaulân, which, however, dries up in summer. A tributary of the same kind, and with a not less quantity of water, is formed by the hot springs which are known by the collective name of el-Hammeh.

The bed of the Sheri'at el Menâdireh is formed in the same manner as that of the great northern tributaries.

Not far from Tell el-Ash'ary the water falls down from the high plateau, over rocky slopes, and flows swiftly between narrow gorges to the 'Allân. Here the valley widens, and is pleasing and fruitful. From Jaulân the northern declivities make a precipitous incline, in several terraces, which are always bordered by lava masses, whilst the river course is embanked beneath a high perpendicular wall of basaltic rocks. The southern slopes of 'Ajlun, in consequence of the chalk formation prevalent there, are less steep. In the Ghôr high earth walls (Arâk Abu Jedeiyeh) bound the course of the river.

The water of the Yarmûk is only a trifle clearer than that of the Jordan, but fresher, and plentifully stocked with carp : thickets of canes, palms, and water plants are found in great variety, and are a favourite resting-place for large numbers of deer and wild fowl, &c.

Throughout its whole course the swift river propels grinding-mills of the most primitive construction, to which the inhabitants of the high plateau bring down corn by break-neck paths. In June, 1885, the Yarmûk, at its union with the Rukkâd, was 50 feet broad, 5 feet deep, with a speed of 4 feet a second. A few hundred feet further below, the river flows swiftly, and at an insignificant depth widens to 100 to 150 feet. In March, 1883, I noticed the enormous mass of water which rolled along in the bed, the breadth of the river near the ford, ½ mile east of el-Hammeh, amounted to nearly 260 feet, and in spite of its great rapidity the water reached to the saddle of my horse.

In the late summer of 1884, the water-mark of the river was higher than in June, 1885, a remarkable phenomenon, which admits, however, of an easy explanation in the difference in the quantity of rain during the two years. The rapid river can only be crossed at those places where fords are indicated ; but even here the saddle-horse constantly stumbles over the bed of smooth polished stones, and has to struggle against the tide with all the force of its strength. Asses for the most part take unwilling baths, which are in the highest degree serious for their riders. If one wishes to travel along the stream from el-Hammeh, it is impossible to avoid frequently crossing the Yarmûk. The route, therefore, is very difficult, and not to be recommended ; beasts of burden cannot in any case manage it.

Besides these streams and wâdies, an inland lake is to be found in Jaulân, named Birket Râm, of which I shall speak in more detail further on. The climate of Jaulân is excellent. Properly speaking, there is no standing water in the high plateau, because the formation of the surface favours an unobstructed flowing off of the water. During the greater portion of the day, fresh west winds blow over the plateau and moderate the heat. The nights are cold, and in the north, especially, a very heavy dew falls, which keeps the first part of the day pleasantly cool. As soon as the sun disappears, the air quickly cools. The influence of the Ghôr is only perceptible on the slopes, for the plateau is elevated at least 1,640 feet above it. It is only the shut-in and perpetually marshy Batîhah and Jordan, near the Lake of Huleh, which engender malignant fevers.

In August and September, 1884, the thermometer on the high plateau of southern Jaulân, at 5.30 a.m., stood on an average at 59° Fah., at its lowest at 55°, but rose during the day to an average of 77°, and at

its highest reached 88° (Jibin, 31 May, 1.30 p.m.). On
May 26 and 27 a light rain fell. In northern Jaulân,
in September, 1884, the thermometer upon the plain
stood in the morning, 5.30 a.m., at an average of 56°
Fah. at its lowest (ed-Delweh, September 17), and rose
to 74° in the course of the day ; it was quite an
exception that on September 14, 12.30 mid-day, with
a strong east wind in the village of el-Kuneitrah,
90° was marked.

With a strong east wind I found southern and
central Jaulân bitterly cold, in December, 1884 ;
whereas in January, 1883, from the 1st to the 4th, it
was mild and agreeably fresh. In June, 1885, the
average temperature of the southern Jaulân was 66°,
at 5.30 a.m., and rose at mid-day to an average of 84°,
whilst at north Jaulân, at the same hour in the morning, it was at 66°, and 77° during the day. These figures
ought to strengthen the rule that it is hotter in the
Jaulân in June and July than in August and September, a phenomenon which is the effect of the proximity
of high mountains. Dew also falls as abundantly in
late summer as in June and July. On the other
hand, in Haifa, as well as in Western Palestine altogether, August is the hottest month. In the Ghôr
(es-Samra), on May 21st, 1885, from 9 o'clock in the
morning to 2.30 mid-day, we registered 98°·6 Fah.
in the shade.

Snow and ice are well-known in the Jaulân.

Except in very mild years, snow falls not only in the
rugged northern part, but also in the south, in the
countries of Fîk, Dabbusch, Kefr Hârib, &c. ; it
remains, however, here for a few hours only, seldom
lying a whole day. In north Jaulân, on the contrary,
it is in the highest degree troublesome to the inhabitants ; for example, for weeks el-Kuneitrah and Jort
el-Hâwa are covered several feet, and compel the
Bedawîn tribes to go further back into the more
sheltered wâdies and ruins. In general, the Fellahîn
consider the limit, down to which the snow falls
regularly and remains lying, a line which runs from
el-Kuneitrah to Joramîyeh towards the southern
bridge over the Rukkâd, and after the bridge, over
the 'Allan (1,640 feet high) ; they call the district north
of this line ej-Jebel, " the mountains," and wrap themselves closer in their thick fur coats at the mention of
the intense cold prevailing there at times.

D.—THE INHABITANTS OF THE JAULÂN.

The people of Jaulân consist of colonised peasants,
Fellahîn, and nomadic Bedawîn (el-'Arab).

The Bedawîn inhabit exclusively the part of
southern Jaulân devoted to corn cultivation, also
the two Zawiyehs, and have established themselves
in the ruins of old places. They have laid the old
basalt building stones upon the top of each other,

without any mortar, and have thus erected their huts ; just as in the olden time the Romans and Arabians employed the smooth, easily split basalt. The roof is supported by rough oak-beams from the prevailing wood of the country. Oleander underwood is laid diagonally and it is then spread over with damp earth and a mixture of clay and fine straw. The walls are, according to the circumstances of the possessor, more or less adorned. The roof of their huts is annually repaired in autumn. The family inhabit the same hut till the roof commences to fall in under the weight of the yearly increasing layer of clay. Then, with the co-operation of the relatives, another hut on another part of the ruins is built. This is the explanation of the many modern ruins found amongst the unrecognisable old ones in the same villages. An exception to this description of buildings are the houses of the sheikhs which serve at the same time as inns, and are therefore better built, and surrounded by a court. Besides the strangers room, or el-Medâfeh, also because it is situated at the top, called el-Ullíyeh, they contain two or three sitting-rooms and a stable. For the summer months the Fellahîn build on the roof of the houses a square or round foliage hut, er-Risheh, made out of branches or reeds woven together, which are used as sleeping-rooms. Such a hut is very acceptable to the traveller, who first learns its value in winter, when he is obliged to pass a night in the dwelling-room itself, which is full of crawling, flying, boring, gnawing vermin.

The fellah of Jaulân is, so far as his field is concerned, industrious, but because he is not used to any hard work he soon fails under too continuous labour, as guide employment for instance. Although inquisitive, like all Orientals, he is nevertheless a well disposed, hospitable man, who, with good arrangement, and discipline, can be made serviceable.

The immoderate inquisitiveness, which with him soon degenerates into obtrusiveness, can be best met by earnest determined dignified behaviour and a few severe but not offensive words thrown at him. Familiarity, if even well meaning, leads to a disastrous result ; the fellah becomes then rude, impudent, and childishly troublesome. The Jaulâner is not badly disposed towards strangers ; he at first exhibits distrust when he is questioned as to the number of souls in the village, the amount of cultivated land, and such things, and increases thus to hostility when instruments and slates are employed, because he fears a new tax. If a man, therefore, wishes to travel comfortably who is not provided with government authorizations, he should avoid making many notes in the presence of the inhabitants. The Jaulâner is tall and well grown, and much browner than the Arabs of Western Palestine ; he has long raven black hair, part of it in a plait and part hanging loose ; and he is clothed in a linen shirt only reaching from throat to knee, to which in winter the well known wool hair cloak, or 'Aba, is added.

The fellah wears a Kuflyeh for head covering, a piece of linen wound round the head in the Bedawin fashion, which is held together by a string ('Agâl) made of goats' hair.

The richness of clothing increases with position and means. If he wears over his linen undergarment a blue cloth coat and a coloured silken cloth for the head, he belongs to the notables of the village or is the village Sheikh himself.

Manâk lâbis jush, ' thou wearest cloth,' is an answer as significant as it is customary when anyone denies that he is one of the Awâdim, the more highly placed (properly noblemen) of the village ; because he is burdened with most of the strangers and soldiers. The Fellahîn's mode of life is extremely simple. The necessary corn for bread he cultivates himself, as well as vegetables (cucumbers and tomatoes), and some water melons. He places much importance on cattle rearing, by means of which he principally lives ; inasmuch as they yield him milk which he uses in both a sweet and sour form ; and also makes into butter and cheese. Rice and meat are dainties ; many have scarcely tasted them, and obtain them only at festival occasions, such as weddings or banquets. In none of the better sort of huts is coffee absent ; it is roasted

in a great iron spoon and pounded in a wooden mortar
with a wooden mallet (Figs. 1 and 2).   If distinguished

Figs. 1 and 2.

guests arrive the Sheikh or proprietor of the Menzûl
prepares a Dabîhah (slaughtered) sheep or kid with
rice and vegetables, which is carried up in a strong
copper dish with freshly baked flat loaves wrapped in
a goat skin.   The guests and most honoured persons
then form a group round the meal, placing themselves
meanwhile on their knees with their body bent
forward.   They then push the hand into the rice
dish, roll some grains up together into a ball and
convey this with enviable dexterity to the mouth.
During the chewing of the food, the dipping hand is
held all the time over the dish, '*Hitta la yeruh esh-
Shasâra,*' 'so that none may fall to the ground.'
Perfect stillness reigns during this proceeding, broken

only now and then by the shout of the host, or
the steps of the attendants, who pour hot melted
butter on the rice heaps, or the el-Humdu el-Allah
rabbet el-'Âlamîn, ' Praise be to God, the Lord
of created things,' from an appeased person, who
rises then to make room for another. The vegetables lie all ready prepared in dishes round the
rice bowls and are eaten by means of the loaves ;
whilst the meat forms a rim on the outer edge of the
rice heap. Each takes as much meat as appears
proper to him ; bites some off and lays the rest back
in its place again. To a specially honoured person it
may happen that a neighbour who has found a piece
particularly soft and succulent, lays it silently on the
place before him, which must be at once consumed
without hesitation and with a grateful countenance.
After the male population of the village is satisfied
and the hands washed and the remains cleared off, a
little coffee (without sugar) which has been roasted
and crushed in the presence of the guests, is handed
round in little doses, two and even three times, as
much as the guest is to be honoured.

Cigarettes and Nafas (water pipes) form the final
enjoyment, to which one yields in pleasant repose
reclining on the carpets.

The women occupy a subordinate position. They
have to attend to the cooking, the making of
butter, the reed plaiting, and such like things.

Polygamy prevails principally in the best (Sheikh) circles ; but the number of wives (four) is, according to instructions, not exceeded. The oldest woman is most anxious to rule, and the youngest to be spoilt by the master of the house. So that neither should get the upper hand, the administration of the domestic arrangements, especially the care of the master of the house by the women, changes from day to day. During her *Dora* (for this arrangement is thus called) each woman is eager to prepare the most dainty portions for the master of the house and win his favour by every possible artifice. So long as the *Dora* of a wife lasts—always one day and one night—the other wives hold themselves aloof from her. Matrimonial morality is severe ; adultery occurs very seldom and brings upon the guilty man the punishment of death.

It is, alas, through this that the avenging of blood, that unhappy legacy from the days of lawlessness, always receives renewed sustenance from the Bedawîn. Marriages are conducted with similar ceremonies and conditions to those of the Fellahîn of Western Palestine. The woman is purchased. The stipulated sum from the bridegroom to the father is discharged by ready cash for the smaller portion of it, and by highly valued cattle for the remaining and larger part. It is considered an honour to increase the sum as much as possible, so that by a silent agreement the real price of the bride is less than the nominal one.

The fellah of the Jaulân and the Haurân is not drawn for military service, but he is compelled to contribute an equivalent sum in money. The Government, by a vigorous mode of action, has not only succeeded in keeping quiet the combative tribes, but has completely subdued them, and made its authority still more regarded than is the case in Western Palestine. The threat of the prison in el-Kuneitrah or Sheikh Sa'âd never fails to have its effect. At the present time, at any rate, there is no longer any question of a.peasant or Bedawin rebellion against the Government. Civil enterprise on the part of foreign Europeans is, therefore, averted as much as 'possible in the beginning, but scarcely indeed in a hostile manner. The Fellahîn, on the contrary, desire foreign capital, and would willingly carry on the agriculture in common with Europeans.

That the inhabitant of the Jaulân and the Haurân is in a very elementary condition as regards education is scarcely to be wondered at. There are no schools at hand, and they are therefore unknown by him. As a purely natural man he is simple and childish, but by no means insensible to novelty. Many times they offered me a cow or a horse for my theodolite in the belief that the distance to favourite spots was

E

marked upon it.   A shepherd who was enchanted
with my telescope immediately offered me his best
coat in exchange, declaring as he used it and
stretched out his hand to the objects appearing
therein, that he would sit on a cliff all day long
and observe the landscape : food thereby he would
not require.   For the rest, the object of the fellah's
desires is the produce of the markets of 'Akka and
Haifa, the fruit transport of which he has occasionally
seen.   As soon as he has a little cash, he quickly
spends it on the things to be got there.   His religion
is Islam, but he is not a fanatic.

Besides the Fellahîn we find in the Ghôr and
Yarmûk valleys four small Bedawîn tribes—the Arab
Segûr el-Ghôr, el-Mukhaibeh, el-Menâdireh, and el-
Kefarât.   The last are partly inhabitants of 'Ajlûn,
and only camp by the Yarmûk during the winter ;
they live in poor tents, and lead a tolerably harmless
existence.   Cattle breeding and a little agriculture
afford them the necessary means of subsistence.

In opposition to the settled Fellahîn of southern
Jaulân we must observe inside the boundary of the
Jaulân the nomadic Bedawîn el-Arab, whose pasture
grounds lie in north-west and central Jaulân.   At
the present day we find there thirteen different names
of clans or tribes, some of which have their pasture
lands definitely allotted, and others by reason of their
relationship possess their land in common.   Besides

these nomads, who ought properly to be reckoned with the settled inhabitants of Jaulân, there are a multitude of other Bedawîn, the tribes of which are related, who come to this rich country during the spring and leave it in the beginning of summer. These are reckoned in the second list because the Government has imposed certain taxes upon them.

From primitive times the Bedawîn or real Arabians of the land of east Jordan have wandered over this tract of country. The pressure of civilization or war has often driven them away ; but they have always managed to regain their old places, and till the most recent times have remained the terror of travellers, for the Government itself was in no position to afford any secure protection. Burckhardt and Seetzen, at the beginning of this century, and other later investigators, suffered greatly from the thievishness and annoyance of the Bedawîn ; but, thanks to the vigorous action of the Turkish authorities during the last thirty years, this nuisance has been put a stop to successfully. The fighting tribes were threatened with extermination, which was, in fact, in part actually effected ; a better administration was given to the Jaulân and the Haurân, and grants of Government with officials and soldiers were founded. Consequently, the traveller of to-day, provided with letters of recommendation from the Government, can travel

E 2

through the whole countries of wide Jaulân and
Haurân unmolested

The large tribes of el-'Anazeh, Ruwalah, have
retired into southern Haurân and the Belka. The
heads of the tribes receive annually a considerable
sum from the Government, and bind themselves
thereby to the preservation of peace. If, however,
a blood feud breaks out, the contending tribes fight
beyond the boundary of Haurân and 'Ajlûn, in the
Hamâd. If, nevertheless, one party retire to this
district the struggle can only be continued by permission of the Government, and this is never granted—
such a retreat signifies defeat.

It was in this manner that the bloody struggle
between the 'Anazeh and Beni Sahkr, in 1885, was
carried on and decided in favour of the latter. In
'Ain Dakar, in the north of ez Zawîyeh es-Shurkîyeh,
of the Jaulân, the 'Anazeh have regularly settled down,
and themselves work the long despised dishonoured
plough-share, instead of investing the surrounding
district with lances and levying a yearly tribute, the
Kuwch, as formerly.

In north-east Jaulân, in el-Kuneitrah, the Circassians drive away the encamping Bedawîn, so that
these latter are limited to the proportionately small
district in north-west Jaulân, of Skêk down to the
Batîhah, and from the Jordan to the western group
of volcanoes.

Here they camp in tolerable peace near each other : *dum* 'blood,' so far as I could learn, is only to be avenged between the 'Arab et-Tellawíyeh of the country near the Batíhah, and their northern neighbour the 'Arab el-Wesíyeh.

This state of things adds considerably to the difficulties of the investigator of these countries, for no guide belonging to one of the tribes can be brought to the frontier places of one of the others.

According to the information imparted to me by the Wesíyeh Bedawín, on whom the expiation devolves, this blood-expiation is a tolerably cold-blooded affair. It is the duty of those belonging to each tribe to watch the steps of the offender : years pass by without any relaxation of watchfulness on either side. At last one of the Tellawíyeh cross the district of the Wesíyeh : his footstep betrays him even in the dark night, and it is then possible, to the devilish joy of the avenger, to shoot him, or stab him, or kill him with a club.

This is such an ingrained vice among the Bedawín tribes that even the Government itself is powerless to oppose it ; indeed, these savage practices will only be restrained when a condition of common social interests and efforts is brought about, and above all by the growth of a sense of national unity.

The Bedawín, as from time immemorial, graze their cattle, churn semen from the milk, which they

sell for a good price to the dealer, or exchange for
linen, spice, and coffee, carry on besides some cattle
dealing and horse-breeding, and cultivate as much
ground as is absolutely necessary for existence.

For the rest they live carelessly, practise the "dolce
far niente" in the most extended sense, and are only
roused by a traveller claiming hospitality, or by
hungry gen-d'armes, upon whom it is laid either to
collect the taxes or summon the Sheikh of the tribe
before the Kada in el-Kuneitrah. Instead of military
service an equivalent yearly tax is imposed upon
them ; on an average the total taxation on a tent of
five persons would be about 120 Government piastres
(1 gold Napoleon = 90 piastres). This is doubled
and trebled according to the opulence of the possessor and the size of the tent, but it is seldom less.

From the 320 tents of the wealthy 'Arab et-Fadel
tribe alone the Government draws on an average
38,400 piastres yearly.

The tent of the Bedawy does not only serve as
a dwelling for the family, but also as an inn. The
spontaneous hospitality which they have inherited as
an obligation from their ancestors is now imposed
upon them as a law, in which, nevertheless, they gladly
acquiesce. They do not make themselves, the cloth
for their tents formed of plaited goat-hair, but for the
most part buy it from certain tribes and gipsies
(Nauwâr), who drive a regular trade in this. The

necessary outlay for this latter is a great grievance to
the Bedawin. The ordinary man possesses a black
tent cloth spread across poles. The wealthy have
threads of white hair interwoven, fasten the tent by
long cords across the poles, and divide it inside into
a roomy reception-room, with carpets and mats, a
strangers' room, and sleeping and sitting-rooms for
the family. As, however, the tent is not able to
withstand the effect of the weather, especially the
snow and cold, the inhabitants of these tent villages
have erected out of the ruined old places which cover
north and west Jaulân, and upon the sites of them,
wretched low stone huts with wooden roofs. Here
they store the in-gathered pasturage and barley, as
well as the straw during the rainy season, and take
refuge therein during the fierce winter weather. These
winter villages consist of from 6 to 30 huts, which in
summer are completely deserted ; they are closed up
by a wooden door made out of a strong oak, and serve
only as haunts for the wild cats and foxes.

The single Bedawin races are detailed below :—

Besides these descendants of once powerful Bedawin
tribes we find (3) in central Jaulân, a large Turkoman tribe, the Arab Turkoman Teljeh, who divide
the pasture ground of the country with the Bedawin.

A branch tribe, Arab Turkoman Suwâdîyeh (with
only 18 tents), leave Jaulân in summer and depart to
the country of Aleppo. In customs and conduct they

differ little from the other Bedawîn, are like all the
other Mussulmen, and, besides Arabic (among themselves), speak a language allied to the Turkish. They
are rather more enlightened, carry on a carpet industry, are of taller, finer stature, and enjoy a more
certain opulence, which, however, does not hinder
them appearing as habitual and dexterous beggars.
Although they are on a tolerably friendly footing with
their neighbours, they preserve the purity of their
race very strictly. Besides which, they have regularly
established themselves in the winter villages of a few
localities where they live entirely to themselves.
Their places, however, are as poor and dirty as the
other Fellahîn villages. Their horses are a more
valuable breed, and their cattle are more prized than
those of the other Bedawîn. As to their past, from
their own lips I could only learn that they had
migrated hither more than a hundred years ago, from
the neighbourhood of Russia, probably from the
Caspian Sea. I am unable to establish the circumstances and motives which led to this.

As in the Haurân so in the Jaulân, the planting of
any kind of flag on the summit of a mountain lying in
the pasture-ground of the tribe concerned, is regarded
by the tribe as a call to arms. I myself had many
opportunities of observing this, because I often had
to put up a signal flag on the prominent heights for
the purpose of trigonometrical measurements.

When I did this, for example, on the Tell esh-Shebân, a portion of the largest tribe of that country, the 'Arab el-Fadel, collected around me in a moment with every description of arms, and asked with an excited air what this signified. Only a detailed explanation and respect for my Government soldiers restrained them from violent action.

The Circassians (Fig. 3) are entirely different from the inhabitants we have considered till now. As a consequence of the Russo-Turkish War, they wandered out of Bulgaria, and in spring, 1878, in a starving and pitiful condition, reached 'Akka, where the Turkish Government assigned them land in Western Palestine, and in Jerash and the Jaulân. By indomitable industry and solid perseverance they soon attained a certain amount of prosperity, built villages, cultivated the fields, bred cattle, dried grass for the winter, and drove the Bedawîn out of their neighbourhood. So that to-day they possess the twelve large flourishing villages in the district of el-Kuneitrah, which are favourably distinguished from the other villages by their cleanliness, size, and solid masonry.

The seat of Government, el-Kuneitrah, is also inhabited, besides merchants and officials, by the Circassians.

In their relations with strangers they are reserved, cunning, and show little hospitality—nay, even are feared as robbers.

The Bedawin well know their courage and spirit.
The pasture grounds have often been the cause of

Fig. 3.

severe encounters, in which the Bedawin, by reason of
their bad weapons and deficiency of courage, were
always defeated.

The consequence of which is that they have to

yield the field and pasture land to the immigrants,
and retire with a vow of eternal enmity. A severe
collision must take place between the tribes ere long,
and it will begin—so the Bedawîn swear—directly
they find a courageous leader amongst them.

As good Moslems, the Circassians are obedient
to the Government, whom they must, in addition,
recognise as their benefactor.

The inhabitants of the north-eastern part of the
Jaulân, in the esh-Shârah, belong to the tribe of the
Druses.

They are likewise more intelligent and industrious
than the Bedawîn. They build fine large villages,
and contentedly sustain themselves on the stony and
little productive soil of the slopes of Hermon and
Jaulân. They live in peace with their neighbours,
but get along better with the Bedawîn than with the
Circassians, who are likewise regarded as intruders
by them. The peculiarity of their religion is well
known.

Finally, in the two villages of Za'ôra and 'Ain Fît,
in western esh-Shârah, close to the slopes of the
Huleh marshes, we find six Ansarîyeh. Long ago
they immigrated from the mountains lying east of
Latakîyeh, in the north of Syria. This industrious
little people have established themselves in three
villages, the two already mentioned and el-Ghajir, in
the plain to the west of Banias. They cultivate

excellent tobacco near these villages, rice at Hulch,
and fruit trees and vines in the lowlands near 'Ain
Fit. Their language is Turkish and Arabian ; their
religion, although originally peculiar to themselves,
now inclines to Islam. They have also put aside
their plundering, cunning character, which I had
opportunities of ascertaining, and are hospitable and
open-hearted. One person in the village is com-
missioned to attend to travellers. This latter (en-
Natûr) provides for the new-comer either at the
expense of the village, or claims Bakshish for his
trouble. They are of middle size and compactly
built, but they have, for the most part, unhandsome
features, and are rather dirty.

In the Batihah we find some poor tents, which
belong to the Kubtiyân, or Ghawârneh, the gipsy
tribe amongst the Bedawîn. Their badly-built little
tents scarcely afford a man lying at full length
protection from the rays of the glowing sun in the
Batihâh. In idleness they roam with the buffaloes
(Jamus), wallowing in the marshes of the plain, upon
whose milk they live, and the proceeds of the cheese
and butter they make. Every year their vegetables
and water-melon culture grows visibly less. The too
tropical sun has an ennervating effect on this little
people, who are on the lowest level of education of
all the tribes and inhabitants of Jaulân. Even the
appearance of the Government gens-d'armes makes

no impression upon them. When we requested them to serve us as guides in the upland country, they regarded me with astonishment for this daring conception of their intellectual capability, as much as to say, ' Friend, you are uselessly troubling yourself so far as concerns us ; our knowledge and capability consists in doing nothing ! ' And they are right.

The population of the Jaulân, including the 1,750 Zawîyeh esh-Shurkîyeh and the portion of the esh-Shârah not marked on the map, should not exceed 11,200 inhabitants of both sexes of ten years of age upwards, if we base our calculation on the populations of the respective places.

If one also adds to this the Bedawîn and gipsies camping within the border of Jaulân, amounting to 8,300, a total of 19,500 is reached, mostly settled inhabitants of Jaulân. The number of Bedawîn who only camp there during the winter amounts to 5,750, according to the list communicated.

E.—ROADS COMMUNICATING WITH THE JAULÂN.

The roads of northern Jaulân have become proverbial, being peculiarly stony and bad. In comparison with those of Haurân, even the most frequented roads may be called untraversable. The paths connecting the winter villages of the Bedawîn are often obliterated between lava blocks, so that

advance is most difficult. But everywhere traces of
the old Roman roads with stone paving are to be
found, which, as they have not been preserved, are,
except in short stretches, entirely in ruins. The
roads leading to the Circassian settlements, by
reason of the better care bestowed on them, are a
praiseworthy exception, so that the two-wheeled
conveyances of the immigrants, although clumsily
enough built, can easily overcome the stiffened floods
of lava. In the north there is a more southerly road,
which, besides connecting the Mejdel esh-Shems and
the Banîas roads of esh-Shârah running from Wâdy
el-Adjam, leads from Damascus across Sa'sa to
Ôphâni (near 'Ain el-Bêda, on the Rukkâd). It then
runs through Merj el-Buk'âti, across el-Mes'adi in
Wâdy el-Khoshabah to the Baniâs, from whence roads
branch off in all directions to Palestine and Lebanon.
Between Ôphâni and the Merj there are distinct
traces of a Roman road. A second one, likewise
running from Sa'sa and Damascus, crosses . the
Rukkâd further south, leads to el-Kuneitrah, and
proceeds past the ruined place, Skêk, to Za'ôra, 'Ain
Fît, and finally to Baniâs. Here, too, are unmistakable
traces of old roads. There is a third principal and
caravan road which follows the above to el-Kuneitrah,
then turns south-west, and goes in a tolerably straight
direction to the southern slope of the Abu en-Nêda
and northern slope of Tell Abu el-Khanzîr; and in

order to reach Jisr Benât el-Yâkûb passes by the
ruined places, el-'Ulleika and Nu'arân, over steep and
very stony ground. It thus bisects upper Jaulân in
the direction of 'Akka and Haifa. This once well-
known and important commercial highway, known in
antiquity and the middle ages as the 'via maris,'
because it connected Damascus with the sea, presents
a sad appearance to-day. It is certainly even now
much frequented, but it is in a very bad state, and
the path—without any detours over lava, cascades,
and blocks of rocks—is a highly perilous one. There
are two other highways, the Sultaneh of Tell el-Hâra
and Damascus, which runs north from Kôdana across
the Rukkâd, and the more southern and principal way
which leads from Nawâ and Haurân over the Rukkâd
to er-Râfîd ; these likewise cross the central part of
Jaulân from east to west. The first takes us across
el-Ghadirîyeh, the second across er-Ruzaniyeh and
Nu'arân by the via maris to Jisr Benât el-Yâkûb. As
it is not easy to cross the Rukkâd by the above
roads in winter, the principal commercial roads of
Damascus are brought over the stone and tolerably
well-preserved arched bridge, Jisr Sueiseh, near
the village of Sueiseh ; they then turn towards
Tell el-Faras across the last-mentioned chief road
of er-Rafîd, and continue in a somewhat southerly
direction across the decaying Khan Jokhadar to
Khîsfin. Here it is joined by the second largest

caravan road of Haurân, which runs from Nawa and
Tsîl across the southern Jisr er-Rukkâd, and united
they take a southerly direction through Zawîyeh el-
Ghurbîyeh to el-'Al and Fîk, from thence, passing
Kefr Hârib to the east, into the southern point of
Jaulân. Here these principal roads turn westward,
run south of the decaying Khan 'Akabeh down the
slopes, cuts through Ghôr south of Tellul es-S'âlîb,
and form a communication with Tiberias across
Semakh, with 'Akka and Haifa across el-'Abeidîyeh
on the Jordan, through Sahel el-Ahma. This, in
reality, is the principal road which cuts through central
and southern Jaulân from north-east to south-west,
having the names of Sultaneh (state road) el-'Akabeh
(after the decaying Khan el-'Akabeh), and is thereby
distinguished from the steep roads leading down
from Derb el-'Arak, and those across Mukatt ej-
Jamûsîyeh, near Kefr Hârib. In autumn this road
is much used by the corn-laden caravans of Haurân;
it is the best road of Jaulân, and in its latter half,
especially through ez Zawîyeh, is broad, smooth, and
tolerably stoneless. Many traces of the old pave-
ment may be found there at this day.

The remaining ways are of slight importance, as is
evident from the map.

The way round the north-east and south coast of the
Lake of Tiberias is very beautiful; but in the Batîhah
one must be careful of the fever lurking near the

shore, and in the hottest time of the day one should never ride along the road. The most beautiful and expansive outlook across the lake and environs may be gained by deviating from the road a little at Kefr Hârib, and posting oneself on one of the roofs of this village. The friendly people willingly point out the various spots to travellers. Their invitation to quarter there for the night should be accepted, for then one can be charmed by a last glance at the departing sun behind the Galilean mountains, and the exquisite changing play of colour in which the coast landscape of the lake is enveloped. Telegraph communication exists up to the present only between el-Kuneitrah, the seat of the Government, and Damascus, and also with Sheikh Sa'ad as the seat of the Governor of the Haurân. The telegraph service in el-Kuneitrah is international, but is worked only in the Arabic and Turkish languages as far as Damascus.

F.—NAMES AND PLACES IN THE JAULÂN, IN ALPHABETICAL ORDER, WITH THE NUMBER OF INHABITANTS OVER TEN YEARS OF AGE.

Abu Ahjar (D. 7).—A small shapeless ruin with scattered stones on a limestone hill in Wâdy Hetal, where the channels of the 'Ayûn Tawarik Hetal springs unite. Here a very luxuriant growth of shrubs

F

flourish, which, however, soon languishes in the bed of the wâdy.

Abu Kebîr (B. 8).—A volcanic hill, covered with great fragments of lava, close to the Yârmûk, where it enters the Ghôr. Its little plateau exhibits regular rows of large unhewn basalt stones, measuring 10 feet square (Fig. 4). On the edge of the square there

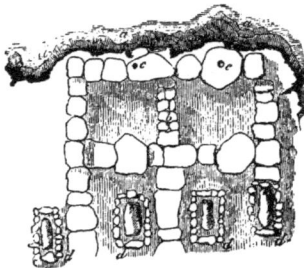

Fig. 4.

Old Stone Wall enclosure in Abu Kebîr.

(*a*) Basalt Rock in the Yarmûk.
(*c*) Cut holes.
(*d*) Bedawîn graves.

are also pieces of wall in single layers devoid of mortar (*b*); these walls are 3 and 6 feet thick. The

single stones are from 3 feet to 4½ feet long, 3 feet
high, and 3 feet thick.

A remarkably large stone lies in the middle and
east and west end of each square. On the upper
side of one of the eastern stones (*c*) a round conically
sunk cavity is carved out, 10 inches deep, whose upper
opening has a diameter of 9 inches, whilst the lower
only 2 inches. The south-eastern corner stone of
another square presents a similar cavity, which is
likewise artificial.

As the whole neighbourhood constitutes a large
Bedawin graveyard, these squares probably indicate
a consecrated place, and even if they do not belong
to hoary antiquity, they are at any rate not modern.

The conical holes were probably intended as re-
ceptacles for libations. Here, from the east and the
south, 'Arabs bury their dead, according to Bedawin
customs, and mark the grave with a large stone. In
these squares, therefore, I recognised the remains of
a very ancient Bedawin cemetery. At the present
day the 'Arab Segûr el-Ghôr, the Beni Sakhr of the
upper Jordan Valley, prefer burying near the Abu
Kebîr, and chisel the mark of their tribe, called
wasm, in the western kerbstone of the tomb. It
was on the tomb of the Sheikh et-Tûka (الطوحى)
formerly head of the tribe of Tuwêk Bedawin (a
branch tribe of the Beni Sakhr), which also bore the
Effendi surname of el-Faiz, that I collected the

F 2

chiselled tribe signs of the Beni Sakhr which are
rendered here (Fig 5).

Fig. 5.

Tribe Marks of the Beni Sakhr.

This tomb lies between Abu Khebîr and Khurbet
Jort ed-Dhahab on the north bank of the Yarmûk in
the Ghôr. These signs consist of the Dabbuseh (club)
 ? (also ٩), el-Buweiter (diminutive of بثر button),
⊕ Shâhid 'witness,' ⁚|, Bâkûra, 'hooked staff' ل, and
Khâtimah 'ring,' or ez-Zenâd ⊙ 'bangle.' The last
is the wasm of the Nu'êm Bedawîn. Whether the
wasm Bâb, 'door,' ∩ which I likewise found there is a
tribe sign of the Beni Sakhr I could not prove with
any certainty. The Arab Segûr el-Ghôr, who came
in the neighbourhood of Abu Kebîr, have chosen the
Bakûra as wasm ; consequently in the upper Ghôr
this sign is found engraved on all the tombs, and in
deserted encampments. This graveyard, extending
from Abu Kebîr to Khurbet Jort ed-Dhahab, over a
fruitful district covered with luxuriant Dôm growth, is

not only interesting on account of its great size
but also on account of its ruined aqueducts and
remains of gardens (ej-Jenîn), and for the collector
of tribe signs it is also a most richly yielding spot.
But the 97° to 99° Fah. of the Ghôr must be
borne !

Abu Rumet (D. 3.)—A very small crater on the
Roman road at the southern foot of Tell Abu en-
Nedâ.

The many springs, pools, and ponds caused this
spot, which formerly lay in the middle of large
Bedawîn encampments, to be a much frequented
rendezvous by the Bedawîn. Here war was declared
or peace concluded : here the lances of combative
warriors were fixed into the earth side by side as a
sign of the peaceful suspension of hostilities until the
feud was resumed at the decision of the heads of the
tribes : here, too, was acknowledged the blood, shed as
an expiation for blood, which had earlier flowed. Ah
yâ Tcherkes ! 'Woe to you Circassians,' called out
my Bedawîn at this explanation, ' You rob us of all of
our memorials, our consecrated places, and drive us
back into the stony wilderness, but—Allahu Akbar !'
(God is great.) Traces of foundation walls, and
many old building stones, prove that Abu Rumêt is
an old site.

Burckhardt (' Ritter, Erdkunst.' xv., Part. I., 168)
mentions a tank, Abu Ermeil, which, according to his

description, agrees with the position of Abu Rumêt which he identifies with Birket er-Râm, which lies much more to the north. Von Schubert also mentions a place, Abu Ermeil, which he calls 'a meeting-place of the people from far parts,' which corresponds with my information about Abu Rumêt. Probably, however, both travellers have erred in the name of the place, for all the Bedawîn were unanimous in calling it Abu Rumêt, and writing it thus, ابو رميت

El-Ahmedîyeh (C. 4), often called also el-Hamedîyeh by the Turkomans. It is a somewhat poorly-built Turkoman village, consisting of twelve huts and seventy inhabitants, west of Selûkiyeh. It lies on a small declivity, at the western foot of which is a ruin, called Shuweikeh. This latter apparently marks the site of the old place, out of which ruins the Turkomans have built their village. Between the two places a fine spring flows, irrigating the vegetable gardens. In the village itself one observes on a stone inserted in a slab, whose inscription (Fig. 6)

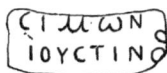

Fig. 6.

Inscription at el-Ahmedîyeh.

has already been mentioned, a Doric capital, and

close by the Jewish nine-branched candlestick, with
the Jubilee year horn (Fig. 7).

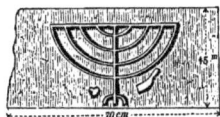

Fig. 7.

Ornament at el-Ahmedíyeh.

This Jewish ornamentation, so prominent at Dannikleh, frequently occurs in the surrounding country,
and leads to the assumption that, in the beginning
of our era, the Jewish people predominated in
western and central Jaulân, as is also testified by
Josephus.

A little beyond the village, in the south of the
mountain terraces, there is a great depression of the
ground, out of which the Turkomans have got up
large hewn and ornamental building stones, because
they have heard a Mâl, a "treasure," lies sunk here.
The basalt stones brought to light present ornamentation in relief which are certainly of Roman origin.
At least, the Roman eagle points to this : its image,
though much mutilated now, has been executed with
great care. My guide, a Turkoman Sheikh, stated
that several more of these Sbâ, "wild animals," had

been raised, but, owing to their enormous weight, had fallen back again, and the treasure, which had already been struck, again covered up (Figs. 8 and 9).

Fig. 8.
Ornament at el-Ahmedîyeh.

Fig. 9.
Ornament at el-Ahmedîyeh.

The building was, therefore, partly subterranean, with, perhaps, a gap leading up from the city to the high-lying fort. The present village apparently covers the old foundations, of which only traces are recognisable.

El-Ahsênîyeh (B. 6).—A ruin of considerable extent in the north of the Batîhah. The rude and hewn building stones are likewise laid with mortar, and, as in el-'Araj, the masonry and chiselling is evidently of Roman origin. The Bedawîn began excavating, and brought to light some interesting pieces of ornamentation, which forcibly remind one of the tombs of the Haurân. They laid bare the building whose ground-plan is given on Fig. 10. It suggests a

Fig. 10.

Building at el-Ahsêniyeh.

bath arrangement. The floor, F, of the principal chamber, consists of two different courses : the upper, 1 to 2 inches thick, consists of a layer of mortar mixed with small stones, known and used even at the present day in Palestine under the name of Barbarîka ; at a depth of 23 inches is a floor of basalt flags. Hence it follows from this, as well as from the enclosure walls, that this building has experienced two architectural periods—that of a Roman and Moslem.

Moreover, the subterranean remains of the neighbourhood, which are furnished with cell-work (Fig. 11)

Fig. 11.

Cell work at el-Ahsênîyeh.

near which pieces of Roman ornamentation are to be
found (Figs. 12 to 14), point to the conclusion that

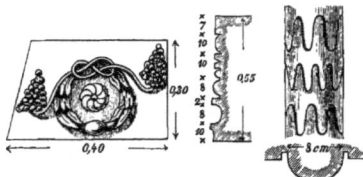

Figs. 12—14.

Fragments of ornamentation found at el-Ahsênîyeh.

they were also built in the Haurân style, for all work
of this kind, $19\frac{1}{2}$ inches high by $19\frac{1}{2}$ inches wide, with
a like depth bridged over by a stone, and forming
altogether a wall $6\frac{1}{2}$ feet high, are to be found all
over the Haurân.

It is to be hoped that the zeal of the 'Arab el-

Tellawíyeh will speedily bring to light some more discoveries.

A second *el-Ahsenîyeh* (B. 4), near el-Fâjer, a small ruin with scattered building stones, and destroyed Bedawîn huts.

'Ain el-'Asal (E. 4).—A fine spring below er-Ruhîneh.

'Ain el-Basâleh (E. 6).—Springs in very stony ground, with some flow to the Rukkâd. In the neighbourhood are dolmens.

'Ain el-Belât (C. 3.).—Several springs, having their source in isolated rock-holes near 'Ain el-Tarîj. The chief spring is clear and fresh, and has a small deep basin with a strong flow, which, however, soon becomes boggy. Here is the chief place of encampment of the 'Arab el-Fadel, particularly the 'Arabs el-Hawaj, whose pasture lands are always green. The country round is the stoniest and wildest part of the Jaulân, because it is here that one of the principal lava streams of Tell Abu en-Nedâ pours forth. Some remains of earlier building near the junction of the numerous springs bear the name of ej-Jueizeh (not the Circassian village ej-Jueizeh).

'Ain ed-Durdara (B. 4).—A bubbling perennial spring on the slopes of the Jaulân, near the Lake of Huleh. Ever-verdant grass and vegetation marks its winding course down the gentle descent to the lake.

'Ain Esfêra (B. 6).—A ruin, with scattered stones and folds for the cattle of the Bedawîn, on a slight elevation of the plateau north of el-'Al. The ruin was once important, but at the present time it is completely destroyed. The spring 'Ain Esfêra lies north of the ruins ; its channel is boggy and deep, with some masonry. Let those to whom this district is unknown be warned of this swampy spring, in whose extraordinary depth one of my companions, along with his horse, was in real danger of his life. In the rainy season it flows into the Wâdy 'Ain Esfêra, and through this down into the wâdies ed-Difleh and Semakh.

'Ain Eshsheh (D. 4).—A fine large spring, the foot of the western slope of Shâfet 'Ain 'Eshsheh a small side spur of the Hâmi Kursu. The spring has a swift flow ; the Seil 'Ain 'Eshsheh forms the beginning of Wâdy el-Wâshâsha.

'Ain el-Fâkhûreh (C. 6).—A winter village, with springs on the eastern slope of the Wâdy es-Semakh.

Only two or three of the persons living in the eight huts, which each contain from six to ten, live there permanently.

'Ain el-Fejrah (B. 8).—A small spring overgrown with reeds on the slope south of Kefr Hârib.

'Ain Fît (C. 2).—A flourishing village of the Nusairich, on the west of esh-Shârah. It comprises sixty huts, and, according to the cramped mode of living of

the people, has about 300 inhabitants. Well-cultivated gardens of fruit trees and vegetables, and a splendid spring, together with tobacco and rice fields in the Huleh marshes, give this village a steady prosperity. The inhahitants are an industrious friendly people. They remember very little of the dwellers of their home in the north of Syria, which they left many years ago.

Unfortunately, on account of the proximity of the Huleh bogs, the place is somewhat unhealthy.

'Ain el-Ghazâl (C. 6).—On the Wâdy esh-Shebib is a small winter village, consisting of eleven huts and some ruins. In summer these huts are inhabited by ten or twelve persons. Near a spring called 'Ain el-Ghazâl.

'Ain el-Ghazâleh (C. 8), in Wâdy 'Ain el-Ghazâleh. —This latter is called in its upper part Wâdy Samâr, and is a large deep valley of 'Ajlûn, which conveys water into the Yarmûk, opposite the Wâdy Mas'âud.

'Ain el-Hâjal (D. 3).—A very small winter village of the 'Arab el-Fadel, with some old building stones and a spring, north of Tell el-Baram.

'Ain el-Hajâra (E. 4).—A boggy spring, without any flow, near el-Breikâh. Around the spring are some stones and ruins.

'Ain el-Hamrâ (D. 2).—A little mud village in a rugged district at the eastern foot of the Tell esh-

Sheikhah. A scanty spring languishes down into the Wâdy 'Ain el-Hamrâ. The village has fallen into complete decay, and belongs at present to the Jebâta el-Khashab (as also the Merj el-Tabel). It is, however, under the administration of el-Kuneitrah.

'Ain Jibîn (D. 7).—Surrounded with good walls, in which the beginning of an arch may still be observed.

The bright clear water runs out of the small superstructure into a sarcophagus, and over it down into the valley. The sarcophagus is of basalt, 6½ feet long by 27½ inches high, and 23½ inches wide. On its longest sides there are two wreaths, like decorations tied with a ribbon, similar to those constantly appearing on sarcophagi. These, however, are defaced and weather-worn.

'Ain el-Katreineh (D. 2).—A boggy spring of bad water, with an insignificant flow, in Merj el-Katreineh, not far from the northern boundary of the Jaulân.

'Ain el-Krûh (B. 7).—A good, clear spring, with a fig tree and a small stream at Mukatt ej-Jâmûsîyeh (west of Kefr Hârib). The country round the spring is overgrown with Abhar (lilac).

'Ain el-Khurj (D. 5).—A tolerably copious spring, with clear water in two rock basins. It has no flow, and is a little north of el-Birch.

'Ain el-Mahyûb (C. 4).—A spring with very little flow, in the valley south of el-Ghadiriyeh, on the Roman road. There are traces of Dolmens here.

'Ain el-Mâlek (C. 7).—A spring with scarcely any flow, beneath the Wely J'afer, near Fîk.

'Ain el-Marshûd (C. 6).—An impure spring on the eastern edge of the Wâdy es-Semakh, with scarcely any flow.

'Ain el-Melekeh (D. 7) the northern, 'Ain et-Bâbi the southern, and 'Ain Jibîn the central, are springs of Jibîn, on the slopes of the Wâdy Hêtal.

All these have plenty of water and some flow.

'Ain el-Mu'allakah (E. 5).—Several springs and puddles beneath the Kulei'âh hills ; the water is muddy but drinkable. They lie in a depression surrounded by sheep folds.

'Ain Musmâr (B. 6).—A remarkably large spring, surrounded by fig trees, on the northern margin of the Batîhah. Its water flows partly past et-Tell into the Jordan, and partly southwards through the Batîhah into the swampy creek Zakîyeh. This second arm is fed in the Batîhah by 'Ain Akel and 'Ain Umm el-Lejjah. Both are fine springs surrounded by fig trees, and used for the irrigation of the Batîhah. The swampy brook is very inconvenient to both horse and rider, and necessitates a detour in the hot glowing plain.

'Ain en-Nakhleh (C. 7), 'Ain Bu'êsteh, and 'Ain el-Beidah, are three springs in Wâdy Mas'âud. Conveying some water even in autumn, they foster a luxuriant growth of brushwood in this

wâdy. At each spring traces of old buildings are found.

'Ain en-Niswân (B. 7), 'Spring of the women ;' 'Ain el-Arâis, ' Spring of the brides ; ' 'Ain er-Rijâl, ' Spring of men ;' and 'Ain el-Kuhleh, ' Spring of the Kuhleh horses,' are four moderately large springs, right under the rocky precipice of Kefr Hârib.

They supply this village with good drinking water. A little brook, the Seil 'Ain en-Niswân, trickles down into the valley.

'Ain Sa'âd (C. 8).—Small ruins, with scanty springs on the northern slopes of the Yarmûk below Dabbûseh.

'Ain es-Semakh (C. 3).—A large spring north of Tell esh-Shebân. It becomes boggy during its flow to the western declivity of Jaulân.

'Ain es-Sidr (C. 7).—A spring with a small stream on the southern slope of the Wâdy es-Semakh, near the ruins et-Tuênni. A side bush dips its roots in the spring, hence its name.

'Ain es-Simsim (C. 4).—A spring on the Roman road, not far from Nu'arân, a Turkoman encampment.

'Ain el-Tarîj (C. 3).—A spring in the stony district of ej-Juêizeh. It flows from a crack in the rock, and has only a very sluggish stream ; but it is copious, and at its source the water is clear and good.

'Ain Tabak Jerjeh (D. 7).—A large spring on the east slope of the Wâdy Hêtal, shaded by three splendid

trees. The name, Jerjeh ('George'), is very rare in this country, and would probably have its origin in earlier centuries, perhaps in the days of the Crusaders. The entire eastern slope of the Wâdy Hêtal is called Tabak Jerjeh ('Declivity of George'). The spring was enclosed, and traces of old masonry were also to be found in the neighbourhood.

'Ain et-Tineh (B. 3).—A plentiful spring above the Wâdy el-Hamd, that flows into the Lake of Huleh. It is shaded by a beautifully grown fig tree.

'Ain Umm 'Otman (B. 8).—A spring with a holy sepulchre, overshadowed by three magnificent trees, on the western slope of the Wâdy Mas'âud.

'Ain Umm Mukhshabi (D. 4).—A feeble spring near a ruin of the same name, north of er-Rumsâniyeh.

'Ain Wurdeh (D. 4).—Fine large springs, north of er-Rumsaniyeh. The springs bubble up out of the ground and flow in a fresh clear brook into the Wâdy er-Ruzaniyeh. They are some of the best and most copious springs of the Jaulân.

El-'Al (C. 7).—A large, well-built village, on the point of reviving. It is close to the fall of the wâdy of the same name, and comprises 65 dwellings, mostly built of stone, with pretty summer huts on the roofs made of willows. The 320 adult inhabitants cultivate the good, stoneless field, of the contiguous high plain, and are pretty well independent of the

G

usurers, who have already most of the villages of the
high plain in their power. In the east of the village
an abundant spring with an insignificant flow. It
has a setting of flag stones. The dwellings of the
Sheikh are spacious and carefully built, and in them
strangers are hospitably entertained by the tribal

Fig. 15.
Basalt Statue at el'Al.

Sheikh, who comes from the most respected old
family of the land.

   The half-forgotten ancient name of the village
seems to have been 'Ain el-Kahwa ; but I cannot go

bail for this information, as it appears only to have
remained in the remembrance of a few old people of
the village. The situation of the village is somewhat
low ; the surrounding territory sinks towards the fall
of the Wâdy el-'Al, which, falling in terraces, presents
wild romantic scenery.

The whole neighbourhood of the village contains
several antiquities of strikingly Roman characters.
In the courtyard of the Sheikh there is a beautiful
statue in basalt, $3\frac{1}{2}$ feet in height : it probably represents a Greek goddess, whose robe, girded round the

Fig. 16.

hips, clings to the body in full folds of drapery
(Fig. 15). In the left hand she holds a shield ; the
right is broken off. Unfortunately, the head is broken

G 2

off as well, and the feet are destroyed by the destructive Bedawin, according to the asseverations of the
Sheikh. In the same courtyard lies a small kind of
sepulchral stone, 31½ inches high, with a Greek
inscription and ornamentation of a rude Doric
character. (Fig. 16a). Its execution is much more
imperfect than that of the statue. The portion
broken off, with the continuation of the inscription
(b), I found set in in the lintel of the door of the
Menzûl. The breadth of the two pieces amounts
to 14 inches. Besides this there are several remains
of basalt columns in the stable belonging to
the Sheikh, certainly only the shafts, no capital,
and here and there a fragment of Roman cornice
(Fig. 17). Beyond—particularly in the east of the

Fig. 17.

village—the inhabitants have discovered a large
number of basalt sarcophagi. Several of them are
entirely destroyed : not one is entirely preserved,
and only one distinguished by good work in high
relief is found on its south side (Fig. 18). A
small head looks out from a medallion, which is
held by two females, whilst in the other hand they

hold up a palm branch as a symbol of peace. Although their heads are destroyed, the curly hair on them is still perceivable. The man's head has also the same kind of hair : his upper lip is covered

Fig. 18.
Side view of Sarcophagus at el'Al.

with a moustache. The execution of the work is artistic, but at the same time not noble. The sarcophagus is basaltic, and 6½ feet long, and 19½ inches broad. Avarice and curiosity will prompt the inhabitants of el-'Al to further investigations, which will result in bringing more discoveries to light.

El-'Amudîyeh (C. 5).—A ruin with a few winter huts on the wâdy of the same name, which joins the Wâdy el-Yehûdîyeh. There is little to be seen now of pillars which have given the place its name.

The position is beautiful; the wâdy falls over high basalt terraces below the ruin. Unfortunately, it was not possible to examine the place more closely.

'Arab ed-Dîab (C. 6).—A Bedawîn tribe, possessing about 120 tents, and camping between Joramâyah and the Wâdy es-Semakh. Formerly prosperous and respected, they are to-day a beggared, degenerated people.

'Arab el-Ekseirîn (D. 6).—In the south of Tell el-Faras, down to the neighbourhood of Khisfîn. The encampment comprises about 80 tents.

'Arab el-Fadel (C. 3).—An aristocratic Bedawîn tribe, which considers upper northern Jaulân as its own. The head of the tribe is an Emir (Prince) who dwells quietly in a splendid tent furnished with costly carpets ; and who receives guests with dignity and pride, begging of them anything that excites his pleasure. The tribe numbers about 320 tents, which are large and small, richly and meagrely furnished according to descent from the family of the Emirs, or cattle-rearers. The former pride themselves on their knowledge of writing, which, however, is of so deficient a nature, that they were only able to comprehend the orders of the Kaimakâms of el-Kuneitrah, when I threatened to set up my tent in the midst of the Sheikh encampment, in the meantime getting orders from the governor which were more within reach of their understanding. A guide was procured finally by grumbling and scoldings, who afterwards displayed so unsympathetic a manner that we were glad when we were able to dispense with him.

They are regarded by their neighbours as a haughty people, and as enemies by the adjoining Circassians. Between the two it has already come to fights, in one of which the father of the present young Emir, the Sheik Shehadi el-Fadel, fell. Since then they regard the Circassians as deadly foes, and the slightest occasion leads to bloody quarrels. Consequently both parties keep carefully apart. Besides extensive cattle rearing and insignificant agriculture, they are now trying vine cultivation, but the attempt made by the Kurm el-Emîr, in the western edge of the plateau not far from Skêk, was certainly anything but promising. The Fadel possess numerous winter villages. A branch of this tribe is the 'Arab el-Hawaj, who graze on the 'Ain el-Belât and at the foot of the Tell esh-Shebân, which is zealously watched and revered by the whole tribe on account of the Emirs buried there. The number of their tents amount to 60.

'Arab ej-Je'âtîn (C. 5).—A tribe whose number nearly reaches that of the 'Arab el-Wesîyeh. They have about 100 tents between Selukîyeh and the Wâdy Joramâyah, and are peaceful frontier neighbours of the Wesîyeh. In former times they carried on a carpet industry, and produced masterpieces in this art by weaving together bright-coloured threads of goats' hair. This industry was exclusively in the hands of the women and girls. We procured a carpet of this kind upon which a girl of the tribe had been engaged

from her youth to her marriage in her 20th year. Certainly a model of perseverance and industry. Altogether, with this carpet, we carried away a pleasant remembrance of the Bedawîn couple; the old woman who had to decide about the purchase of the carpet, raised it up several times, announcing finally, "If you will add two Mejedies (9 francs) to the prime cost, so that I can purchase a respectable honourable tomb for my tribe-comrades, you can take it away." And so it happened.

'Arab el-Kefarât (C. 8), or el-Ekfarat.—The Bedawîn of Kefarât, the north-eastern district of 'Ajlûn. They are partly Fellahîn, who in spring only pasture their cattle and cultivate the slopes in the valley of the Yarmûk from el-Mukhaibeh to the Rukkâd; but who in summer and winter withdraw to the plateau of 'Ajlûn, only passing a few weeks in the valley at harvest time.

'Arab el-Menâdireh (D. 7).—The Bedawîn tribe from which the Yarmûk gets its name of Sheri'ât el-Menâdireh. They are a thrifty industrious little people, who have established themselves in the valley of the Yarmûk, upon whose slopes, from the Rukkâd upwards, they graze and plant. Like all the Bedawîn tribes of this valley they are under the jurisdiction of the 'Ajlûn, and in certain details also that of the Haurân (see Schumacher's 'Across the Jordan,' 4, 12, &c.)

'Arab el-Mukhaibeh (C. 8).—A small poor Bedawîn

tribe, with hardly 30 tents. Their cattle feed in the valley of the Yarmûk, from ed-Duêr upwards to the hot springs of el-Mukhaibeh, on the Yarmûk. Their sheikh, Kâid, considers himself the owner of the great palm-wood at el-Mukhaibeh, which in its way is a unique phenomena of the east Jordan valley. In the bathing season (April and May) the tribe furnish the hundreds of bathing visitors in el-Hammeh with sheep, goats, and vegetables. The tribe is under the jurisdiction of Irbid in 'Ajlûn.

'Arab en-Ne'arneh (B. 4) have 70 tents in the country of Nu'arân and el-'Ulleika. They cultivate corn, and, as second crop, some Italian corn (dura Safra), which they water and guard with Argus-eyes ; for, during the hot season of the year, travellers as well as cattle are glad to consume the knots or stalks for refreshment.

'Arab en-Nu'êm (E. 5), or en-Nu'êm el-Yûsef. A large wealthy Bedawîn tribe, which is spread over east Jaulân and north Haurân to Nawa. The number of their tents in Jaulân amount to 280 ; their head-quarters in summer are at Tell el-Faras, whose country, rich in springs, is well suited for their great herds of cattle. According to the latest orders, the Government is driving them out of this country, because they wish to keep the luxuriant pasturage for their own flocks in Damascus. So the Nu'êm, with sad countenances, retire eastward, always further away

from the alluring Belâd er-Rabî, of which the Government officials have seized possession and only left a
part to the Circassians. The Nu'êm are peacefully
disposed, and friendly to strangers, and indulgent to
the Wesîyeh Bedawîn, who serve them (*see* above); in
them the Jaulân loses its best Bedawîn tribe. The
tribal mark of the Nu'êm has the Khâtima ○ be-
tween two strokes | |, el-Matârik (Sing, Matrâk),
consequently the following *wasm*, | ○ |; the two
strokes signify lances driven into the ground, the
sign of truce.

A small branch tribe of the 'Arab en-Nu'êm el-
Yûsef are the *'Arab es-Sebârdjah* (D. 4), who occupy
about 25 tents in the country of er-Rumsanîyeh.
They cultivate some land and rear cattle.

'Arab er-Rekêbât (B. 7) (or Erkêbât), the " owners "
of the Wâdy es-Semakh.—This small Bedawîn tribe
of about 80 tents has established itself principally
in the valley, and built a few miserable huts out
of the ruins. Their head-quarters are found at the
winter village of el-'Adêseh. Besides, they cultivate
a portion of the east coast of the Lake of Tiberias,
and are consequently in part tributary to the Kada
Tûbarîya. They are a poor but friendly people,
although malicious tongues aver they are unable to
leave off their unpleasant vagabond habits. But they
are by no means bloodthirsty, and are contented with
little. On their account the east shore of the lake

is in somewhat bad repute, and not unjustly, if they are the same of whose robbing propensity Seetzen has already spoken ('Ritter Erdkunst.' xv., 272).

'Arab Segûr el-Ghôr (B. 8).—A branch tribe of the Beni Sakhr, who, in earlier times, possessed the upper part of the Jordan valley, but have now been driven further south. At the end of the last and beginning of this century they were the most fearful robbers, and even to-day, the booty-loving Segûr el-Ghôr give the Kada Tûbariya, to whom they are tributary, plenty of work.

'Arab es-Siyâd (B. 4).—On the east coast and slopes of the Huleh Sea. They are a small tribe ; I counted about 40 tents ; but there is possibly another portion of it in the lowlands of the Huleh Sea.

'Arab et-Tellawîyeh (B. 6).—This tribe camps in the Batîhah, and on the low slopes bounding it on the north. They grow corn, grain, and vegetables on the plain ; and in the rainy season withdraw to their winter villages, et-Tell and el-Mes'adiyeh, in the Batîhah, and er-Rafîd on the Jordan, a part also to ed-Dikkeh. Their name is derived from the village et-Tell, and they have about 50 tents, whose inhabitants in Batîhah are under the jurisdiction of the Kada of Tiberias, whilst the other villages are under that of el-Kuneitrah.

'Arab Turkomân Teljeh (C. 4).—A Turkoman tribe of the Jaulân. The 300 tents which they possess are

on the whole somewhat better than those of the
Bedawîn Arabs; their draperies, also, with a design
imitated from the Persian, differ from that of the
goat-hair carpets found in the Bedawîn tents, although the Turkoman formerly supplied the Bedawîn
with carpets. They have numerous flocks of cattle,
which are valued less for their race and milk than as
fatted cattle, which are excellent and much sought
after. Besides this they possess a noble breed of
horses, the best of all, except those of the 'Anazeh
Bedawin of the Haurân. The chief Sheikh declared
to me that he had recently sold a snow white mare
for 1,000 Napoleons, in ready money. Their head-
quarters are situated on the beautiful spring of el-
Ghadirîyeh, but several families have permanently
settled themselves in the villages. Their winter villages in the Jaulân are, like those of the Bedawîn,
miserable quarters. They are also great beggars, and
never hesitate when occasions arise to compound to
their own advantage 'mine and thine.' Consequently
these great bearded individuals do not inspire a traveller
with much confidence, but they are very hospitable.

'Arab el-Westyeh (B. 5).—As has been already said,
this Bedawin tribe lives in blood feud with the tribe of
the Tellawiyeh, a state of things productive of great
unpleasantness to the visitor of these close lying
districts.

They graze on a narrow strip of central Jaulân, from

the east of Jordan to Ghâdir en-Nuhâs, are fairly big cattle rearers, and have 120 tents. A small part has separated from the tribe, drawn off eastward, and pasture their cattle on the land of the great tribe of the 'Arab en-Nu'ĉm at Tell el-Faras, in return for which they give a share of the stock. During the rainy season they withdraw to a number of winter villages, but their head-quarters remain at 'Elmîn.

'Arâk Abu Jedeiyeh (B. 8).—Steep earth walls on the Yarmûk below Khirbet Jort ed-Dhahab in the Ghôr, which are formed by the bed of the river becoming gradually deeper.

'Arâk el-Ahmar (C. 8).—A rugged precipice with basaltic heaps on the northern slope of the Yarmûk, west of Dabbûseh.

'Arâk el-Arrâbeh (B. 8).—The northern slopes of the Yarmûk, not far from el-Hammeh, which fall in terraces from Sahel el-'Arrabeh, on the high plateau, to the river.

El-'Araj (B. 6).—A large, completely destroyed site, close to the lake in the Batîhah. The building stones of basalt are unusually large ; also the foundations, which are still visible, and are built in part with white mortar. A group of palm trees stands south of the ruin, and dips its roots in the mud of the damp marshes, over which the traveller is brought by an old stone path. It is not possible for riding animals to cross it, for the stones have become so loose, and no longer permit a firm footing. But as there is a threatening morass 6½ feet deep on each side of the old dam, they must pass on the upper part of the plain. This dyke is the remnant of an old practicable Roman road, whose traces can be followed from el-'Araj to et-Tell.

For several years a large well-built corn magazine has stood on the ruin. It is the Hâsil of the famous leader of the Mecca pilgrims, Muhammed Sa'îd Pasha, who, beside his religious claims, has also a large interest in the finest and most lucrative strip of land of the Jaulân and Haurân, and over these rules with almost unlimited power, and free from all taxes. He is also the owner of a part of the Batîhah. In the neighbourhood of this magazine the Bedawîn of the plain are encamped : here the Kubtiyân idle, here the fishermen from Tiberias land and mend their nets, here also the traveller finds a guide for the country most easily, and in wet weather finds excellent lodgings with the manager of the magazine, unless the latter is absent in Tiberias for purposes of recreation at that particular time.

Ard el-'Alâ (C. 7).—West of el-Yâkûsa, bordering the Ard el-Rummaneh.

Ard el-Balû'a and 'Ain el-Balû'a (C. 2).—The country and springs in the north of stony Jaulân. The country is so called — Bâlû'a means abyss, grave—because it was the scene of bloody feuds between the villages of Skêk and Summâka at the time when these were still inhabited. The Bedawîn still speak with horror of that period, scarcely a generation back. The spring is perennial and irrigates some vegetable gardens near Kurm el-Emir.

Ard el-Ekhdeiyil (B. 6).—A stony district of land in the Batîhah near el-Ahsêniyeh.

Ard el-Huleh (B. 3).—The whole country of the marshes of the Huleh Lake, a swampy territory thickly overgrown with papyrus. It abounds in snipe, wild ducks, francolins and many other kinds of birds, and is consequently much resorted to by the hunter, but as carefully avoided by the inhabitants on account of the noxious fever.

Ard er-Rummâneh (C. 7).—The plain south-east of Fîk, formerly a pomegranate tree garden (Rummân).

El-'Arêt (B 6).—The bald terraced mountain ridge which extends from el-Lâweh, in the north of the Wâdy es-Semakh towards the lake. According to its position and nature, and leaving Gadara out of the question, it corresponds to the place mentioned in the Bible where the swine ' ran violently down a steep place into the sea' (Matt. viii. 28), because the precipices fall more ruggedly here than anywhere else on the east coast of the lake ; and, moreover,

Kursi, which nominally corresponds to the Biblical
Gergesa, lies at the foot of this fall.

'Arkûb et-Tintyeh (B. 8).—Also a part of the
northern slopes of the Yarmûk, not far from
ed-Duer, terminating in a circular cone.

El-'Aselîyeh (B 5).—A ruin of unusual extent,
with an enormous number of large hewn and unhewn
building stones, giving evidence that at one time this
place was of great importance.

The meaning of the name, "place of honey," does
not bring us any nearer to the history of the old
place ; and the ruins, so far as I could judge in a
hasty examination, do not point to any definite
period of architecture. Mid-way below them is the
grave of the Sheikh Mûsa, who is so much honoured
that the place is known by the collective names of
Sheikh Mûsa wa'l-'Aselîyeh. I am, however, unable
to fix the age to which this Moslem saint belongs.

West of the ruins, where the basalt terraces make
a fall, we saw traces of a firm city wall, built of
powerful rude squares, which surrounded the lower
portion of the town, where a beautiful plain stretches
against the lava terraces. At the foot of the latter,
the clear abundant spring, 'Ain esh-Sheikh Mûsa,
bubbles forth from a solid stone setting built with
white mortar ; it irrigates the environs. There is
also here a Mazâr or memorial of the Sheikh Mûsa
shaded by large and very old terebinths and oaks.

Other building remains, and large hewn stones present themselves in the neighbourhood.

'Atâlî ed-Duêr (B. 8).—Perpendicular basalt walls at the ruined village of ed-Duêr which bound the course of the Yarmûk.

El-'Awânîsh (B. 7).—Ruins of a village with some old remains and a good strong spring on a level and very well-sheltered spot, immediately below the steep upper walls of the Wâdy es-Semakh. The spring, 'Ain 'Awânîsh, flows from the Wâdy es-Semakh and irrigates the ground near the bottom of the valley. At the foot of the slope below the ruin there is an isolated lime-stone hill, with a solitary well-built winter hut belonging to the 'Arab er-Rekêbât, called Ferj 'Awânîsh. The mountain ridge above the ruin is also called el-Awânîsh. According to the statement of the natives, the place was once important, and this is confirmed by the fact that the same name is attached to several places in the neighbourhood ; but all the same, the place cannot have been of great extent.

El-'Aweinât (D. 2).—Three springs, without any flow, close to the northern border of the Jaulân ; the water is bad, and is used only for the flocks.

'Ayûn (B. 8).—A ruined village in the southern extremity of the Jaulân plateau, on the western margin of the Wâdy Mas'ûud. The old settlement covered a space of several hektars, and presents traces of different

H

masonry of modern, mediæval, and ancient times. A
number of large, mostly unhewn, basalt stones lie
heaped up between the falling huts of a Bedawîn
winter village ; the foundation walls of buildings in
Moslem times, and Roman remains in the form of
basaltic shafts of columns, still exist ; these last
measure 5 feet in length, and 12 inches across. There
are also some old subterranean corn magazines with
traces of basalt roofing. An old basalt stone, 28
inches long, at present the door-post of a small hut,
bears the Greek inscription of Fig. 19. In any case, at

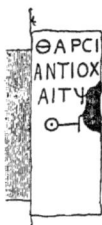

Fig. 19.

Inscription on door post in 'Ayûn.

one time, the place must have been important. On
account of its position it commanded the outlet of
the Wâdy Mas'âud and the valley of the Yârmûk,
with the country of el-Hammeh. The head of the

valley falling eastward is called Wâdy 'Ayûn,
lower down, where it joins the Yârmûk, Wâdy el-
Mugheiyir. While I was stopping there a band
of Ghawârneh gipsies had several donkeys yoked
together, treading out the maize, whilst the women
cooked beneath the open sky, and some half-grown
impudent youths busied themselves in bringing the
threshed-out maize into one of the old corn store-
houses of 'Ayûn. Others made faces at us. Maize
flourishes excellently on the southern plateau.

'Ayûn el-Fahm (D. 5).—A number of fine springs
at Tell el-Ferj, whose waters irrigates the upper
Joramâyah.

'Ayûn Mukhladi (C. 4).—Large running springs
above el-'Ulleika. The clear stream contains excellent drinking water and flows into the Wâdy Kêfr
Naphakh. One arm of the stream crosses the
Roman road and flows in a curve below the Wely
Marzûk, likewise into the above mentioned wâdy,
after having been already used to irrigate the Italian
corn. The lower portion of the springs bear traces
of masonry, aqueducts, &c., which, however, may very
likely be modern.

'Ayûn es Suwân (D. 3).—A large Circassian village
near el-Kuneitrah, situated on both sides of the spring
and pool of the same name in the midst of a beautiful
and fertile plain. It is bounded on the west by Tell
Abu en-Nedâ, and in the east by the spurs of the

H 2

Hâmi Kursu. The village comprises at the present day 100 buildings, with about 450 inhabitants above the age of 10 years. The buildings are composed of basalt stone, without any mortar, but the walls are firm and solidly built. Each dwelling-house, with its little vegetable garden, is encircled by a court.

On an open place bordering the spring is the Mosque, shaded by willows, never absent from a Circassian village. The whole conveys an impression of industry, order, and cleanliness. In opposition to the dirty narrow streets of the Fellahîn villages, which wind irregularly between the huts and ruins, and which are beset with lazy Arabs, we find here broad straight streets, filled with active busy figures, always on the alert to repair damages, and build up anew what is necessary. There are heaped-up hay-cocks, reminding one pleasantly of home, and creaking two-wheeled carts are drawn over the even streets. If only the faces were in harmony with the peaceful conduct! Instead, one sees nothing but wild, forbidding, malicious faces, and a stranger scarcely ever receives a friendly greeting. The graveyards also outside the village are carefully kept.

No ancient remains are to be found. The village only arose about 7 years ago, and was only arbitrarily designated by the officials in el-Kuneitrah according to their own admission. But there lies, here and there, some old building stone that has come from the walls, and we might perhaps have been able to discover some name, handed down by tradition, if the Bedawîn had not been driven away.

The Circassian villages increase rapidly. 'Ayûn es-Suwân, for instance, a year ago had only 60 dwelling houses. The population increases with the extension of landed property and the clearance of the ground from bushes and stones.

'Ayûn Tawârik Hêtal (D. 7).—Eighteen moderately large springs on the north and eastern slopes of the Wâdy Hêtal. Oleander and kuseb (cane) bushes mark out their course down the slopes.

'Ayûn et-Tôm (D. 4).—Several large springs which discharge into the Wâdy Selûkiyeh. The 'Arab es-Sebârdjah encamps in the neighbourhood of them.

Ayûn Yûsef (D. 4).—Three fine springs at the foot of the Tell Abu Yûsef. They flow into the Wâdy ed-Delhamiyeh.

'Ayûn ez-Za'ôra (E. 5).—Numerous springs at the foot of Tell el-Faras ; is one of the principal encampments of the 'Arab en-Nu'êm. As the country is tolerably stoneless, gardens can be laid out without much trouble.

El-'Azarîyeh' (B. 2).—Also called el-'Ozeîriyât, a village in the plain of Baniâs, which I did not visit.

Bâb et-Tumm (A. 8) is the name given to the southern mouth of the Jordan from the Lake of

Tiberias. During the largest part of the year a
boat is kept there ready to transport animals and
baggage.

Baheiret el-Huleh (B. 4).—This lake measures at its
greatest length 3½ miles, and 3 miles at its greatest
breadth. The measurements vary considerably in
consequence of the low swampy bank, and also according to the amount of rain during the year. As
another consequence the form of the lake, more
especially in the north, where several arms of the
Jordan discharge, is not always the same. Altogether
the lake is pear-shaped in form, with its largest curve
on the west coast and a sharp point on the south.
The east coast is luxurious for the growth of plants,
but gets somewhat boggy in the north. Its level is
only about 7 feet above the Mediterranean Sea.
(Western Survey, P.E.F.). The district is hot and
malarious but the favourite resting place of the
water-fowl. The Baheiret el-Huleh is identified
with the Lake of Hermon of the Old Testament, and
Lake of Semechonitis of Josephus.*

---

* It is customary to identify the Lake Huleh with the 'waters
of Merom' (Jos. xi. 57), but this is neither capable of proof
nor probable. It should be observed that Josephus ('Ant.,'
V. i. 18) places the spot where the defeat of Jabin at Beroth
took place in Upper Galilee, and consequently does not look
for it in the Jordan lowlands. Instead of the Lake of Semechonitis, according to Josephus (4 Wars. I. 1), it is ' Lake of
the Semechonites,' viz., of the inhabitants of the district of
Semechonitis, or of a place called Semechon.

Bahr Tubarîya.—The Lake of Tiberias. The whole coast district is under the administration of the Kada Tûbariya. From its inlet to its outlet the lake is nearly 13 miles long and 5½ miles broad from Tiberias to Khirbet el-'Âshek, on the east coast. It reaches its greatest width several miles north of Tiberias and tapers somewhat at each extremity. Rather more south than the Jordan mouth lies Semakh, so that the greatest length of the lake is 13 miles exactly. At Semakh its southern end forms a beautiful rounded bay, which is enclosed by earth walls from 16 to 33 feet high ; whilst the northern end east of the Jordan has a very flat coast, penetrating with bays and creeks into the swampy Batihah.

Whilst the western coast is rocky and stony, the entire east coast bounds a fine fruitful plain about 878 yards broad (see Fig. 20, and View of Wâdy es-Semakh). On the eastern edge of this plain the Jaulân slopes begin to rise steeply. A gravel stratum lies immediately on the east coast. With the exception of the Wâdy es-Semakh and the Wâdy Fîk or Enghib, which have abundant water in winter, but dried up in summer, there are only a few small wâdies which feed the lake from the east. In summer it is only the afflux of the Jordan and a few small streams on the western coast which feed the lake ; consequently the surface of the water, which, according to the Survey of Western Palestine (P.E.F.), lies 6,825

feet beneath the level of the Mediterranean Sea, sinks
and rises somewhat according to the season of the
year.

The fluctuations may easily be recognised on the
white deposit marks on the town walls of Tiberias.

Mouth of W. Fîk.   El-Kuweiyir.   Kurein Jeradeh.

Fig. 20.

View of eastern shore of Sea of Galilee.

My observations at different times of the year yielded
the result that the greatest fall for many years was
obtained on December 17th, 1884, in consequence of

the lack of rain. The water stood at that time $4\frac{1}{2}$ feet lower than on the 4th January of the same year, $20\frac{1}{2}$ inches lower than on February 27th, 1884, and $14\frac{1}{2}$ inches lower than on September 28th, 1884. The water of the lake is sweet and tolerably clear. Storms and sudden currents, with bounding waves, are not uncommon, so that a journey across in spring and winter, with bad sailing boats unskilfully guided amongst the ships of Tiberias, is not always unattended with danger. In summer the heat on the lake and surrounding region is rather too depressing, consequently one should always choose the very earliest hours in the morning for riding and working. The lake contains a quantity of eatable fish of all descriptions, which are named in the volume treating of the Flora and Fauna of Palestine in the English 'Survey of Western Palestine' (P.E.F.). Also crabs, and in winter many sea-fowl, principally wild ducks and water hens, enliven the shore. The east coast was formerly covered with towns and buildings, as is proved by the numerous ruins. To-day there are only two villages still standing, Semakh and es-Samra. At the foot of the mountain Moka'adla several sulphur springs break out on the coast; they are called el-Hammeh, and have a temperature of 105° (at an atmospheric temperature of 94°), and each pour forth about 4 gallons of water a minute.

This small quantity soon trickles into the gravel,

whereas by a proper enclosure of the spring it could
be easily kept together.

El-Batîhah (B. 6).—The ordinary name for the
charming plain surrounded by gentle slopes on the
eastern edge of the Lake of Tiberias. Its extent
between the Jordan and the ruin Duket Kefr 'Akib
is 4 miles: between the mouth of the Wâdy Joramâyeh and its entrance into the plain is 3 miles,
whilst its breadth in the centre reaches only 1½ miles.
The ground, probably a part of the old lake basin, is
muddy but rough, and owing to the deposits of four
large rivers which convey their silt and discharge
themselves into the plain, it has become more and
more raised.

The plain is sown two or three times during the
year by the 'Arab el-Tellawîyeh, and grazed by the
buffalo herds of the Ghawârneh, or Kubtiyân. Numerous large springs break forth on the northern edge:
the water is used by the Bedawîn to irrigate the fields
after the first corn harvest in June, in which they
then sow Indian corn. When this is gathered in they
plant vegetables and water melons. All three har-
vests yield abundant produce. In its lower part on
the Lake the Batîhah is very marshy; the Lake
breaks deeply into the land (Zakîyeh), making the
coast completely untraversable. In its north-western
part the plain is covered with ruins, most of which
are of fair size. The Bedawîn have constructed

winter huts out of the old building stones. The Batîhah is poor in tree growth : this only begins on the northern edge. Wild figs, Pomegranates and Dom, are to be found in the neighbourhood of the springs : palms and fruit trees in el-Mes'adîyeh and el-'Arâj. As to the aloes mentioned by earlier travellers, only stunted remains are now to be seen in the burying-ground of et-Tell. The temperature of the plain is a very high scorching one, like that of the Jordan Valley, and during the south wind especially is nearly unbearable. Add to this the marshy ground on the coast it will be seen that the climate of the Batîhah is an unhealthy one, and breeds fever. By proper drainage this nuisance could be somewhat lessened, and, at the same time, the productiveness of the soil increased.

Bêdarûs (C. 3).—A large ruin in stony Jaulân. Although there are no huts, nor a single entire building to be found at this place, there are a great number, mostly unhewn, of large building stones on square foundations to be found here, that it is evident this is the site of a well-built town of considerable size and great antiquity. These ruins have fallen together in heaps, and lie in such confusion that nature, probably by an earthquake, must have contributed to the work of demolition. There are traces of an old road leading from Têlestân right through the ancient site southwards to the Roman road. Further distant

we find old burial places which are overlaid with
basalt slabs, and also large subterranean rooms, 13
and 16 feet square, which are enclosed by blocks of
basalt still standing, and were originally roofed with
the same material, but are now exposed and ruined
owing to the avarice of the Turkoman. The walls
measure, so far as is visible, from 30 to 40 inches
in thickness. The following diagrams illustrate the
arrangement of the layers (Fig 21). The gaps are not

Fig. 21.

Layers of Basalt Stone Wall.

filled in with mortar; nevertheless they are never
wider apart than one-third of an inch at most, and the
stones are unhewn. As for ornamentation, I found
a column or capital in the Haurân style (see Jibîn
and Kuneitrah), and a simple rectilineal cross on a
pyramid-shaped stone lately dug up. From that it
may be concluded that there was once a Christian
settlement at this place. If once the rubbish was
cleared away and the foundations laid bare, there is
no doubt that the veil over the part of this, as well
as many other large ruins of Jaulân, would be lifted.

Ben et-Tellul (B. 8).—The country between the Tellul es-S'âlib and the slopes of southern Jaulân, not far from the southern bay of the Lake of Tiberias. It forms a proper continuation of the east coast of the lake—a fruitful tract.

Bîr ej-Jekûm (B. 7).—A miserable village, consisting of thirty-one huts, built out of basalt and clay, situated on the western slope of Jaulân, near Skufiyeh. It contains 150 inhabitants. The Fellahîn cultivate the slopes and some land on the east coast of the lake.

Bîr el-Ajam (E. 4).—A large Circassian village on the Hami-Kursu, consisting of separate parts. It is built in the same sort of way as 'Ayûn es-Suwân, comprises at the present day about eighty huts, and according to the nominal census 340 souls. A fine spring lies in the north, and another near a pond in the south, of the prosperous village.

Bîr el-Kabak (D. 5).—Several perennial springs in Wâdy Selukîyeh. From here downwards the valley is called Wâdy Bîr el-Kabak.

Bîr et-Trûh (D. 7).—A large pool with a spring, on the road by the village Hetal. Beautiful oleanders grow.

El-Bîreh (D. 5).—A winter village of twelve stone huts and several ruined ones, in the possession of the 'Arab ej-Je'âtin. A number of large unhewn building stones lie round a very old Butmeh (terebinth), which shades the grave of a saint and a Bedawîn grave-

yard. Between them traces of rectangular foundations present themselves. The ruins cover an area of
about 64 acres, consequently the place was not unimportant. The name may possibly be explained by
the Aramaic signification of 'Fort Castle ;' we have
then the alternative of recognising in the ruins of an
old fort, or that the name refers to a colossal cleaved
block of rock, a fragment of the burnt lava stream
which lies in proximity to the terebinth. North of
the place the good spring 'Ain el-Bîreh flows, conveying its water to the Wâdy el-Bîreh, and runs in a
narrow stony channel into the Wâdy el-Yehudîyeh,
but takes before the junction the name of Seil el-
Kurdîyeh.

Birket el-Ekfeir (C. 2).—A large natural reservoir,
north of Za'ora, supposed to have been a spring.
From here one can obtain a wonderful view over
Baniâs, its castle, and the upper course of the Jordan.

Birket ej-Jarab (B. 8).—See el-Hammeh.

Birket Râm (D. 2).—A small inland lake of northern
Jaulân, called by the inhabitants of Mejdel esh-
Shems, Bîrket Râm; by the inhabitants of the Druse
villages, el-Buk'âti and Jebata el-Khashab, its name
is Bîrket Rân. Thus both names are usual. In
June, 1885, the lake measured at its greatest length,
from south-east to north-west, 690 yards, and at its
greatest breadth, near the middle, 523 yards.

Its circumference is about 1,744 yards ; in the east

its long rounded form has a small bay. The lake
evidently fills up the mouth of a crater.

It has neither affluents nor effluents on the surface, but is enclosed by steep crater walls of earth
and basalt rocks, which rise to 200 feet above the
level of the water ; this belt is highest in the south,
sinks towards the north, and is lowest in the north-
west. The rear of the belt, which makes a fair circle
round the Birkeh, is extraordinarily narrow, and falls
off sharply outwards, so that the crater stands somewhat isolated. It is only in the south that the slope
of the Krum et-Turkoman comes quite close to the
walls of the crater ; on the other side it is bordered
by the Merj el-Yafûreh. The water-mark of the
lake very much depends on the amount of rain of
the year, so that the form and size fluctuate. This
observation is confirmed by the fact that when the
above measurements were made, a narrow plain of
from 50 to 70 feet between the brink of the water
and the slope was left, and traces of an expanded
surface of water were visible upon it. The coast and
an inner strip, 70 to 100 feet, are overgrown with
swamp vegetation, in which numerous gorgeous toads
move about. Near the shore the water is clear and
pleasant tasting, and has no brackish after-taste ; its
temperature is 77° Fah. at an atmospheric temperature of 81° Fah. In the middle, where the water is
free of any kind of plant growth, there is, according

to the unanimous testimony of the natives, a whirl-
pool, to which they would only venture by dint of
tremendous promises. As we had no boat at hand
we were unable to test their statement, or to settle
whether the lake basin in the centre is really of un-
fathomable depth. Fish are not to be found in the
lake, but I observed some beautiful large blackish-
green turtles. Numerous sweet springs break out
on the coasts, but their slight flow does not nearly
replace the daily evaporation.

Consequently, one may conclude with certainty
that there are subterranean channels or springs,
because, in the absence of these, the water of the
lake dependent on the rain for replenishment would
lose its clear freshness. The surface of the water
lies 3,360 feet above the level of the Mediterranean
Sea. On the shore we find huts of underwood and
earth, which serve the inhabitants of Mejdel esh-
Shems as places of ambush for duck-shooting in
winter. These birds appear in such large flocks, that
on the shore at nights they can be knocked down
dead with sticks.

Birket Râm must be identical with the Lake Phaila
of Josephus (3 Wars, X. 7), because its position, as
well as form, corresponds with the statement of the
Jewish writer. But his assumption, and that shared
by his contemporaries, that the lake is the real
source of the Jordan, is no longer considered worth

any one's serious notice. (As regards Burckhardt's confusion of Bîrket Râm—not er-Râm—with 'Bîrket Hefah,' see under Kefr Naphâkh.)

El-Breikah (E. 4).—One of the largest and best of the Circassian villages at the northern foot of the Tell el-'Akkâsheh. It contains more than 100 houses, 85 families, or about 425 inhabitants, amongst them 68 fighting men. This village, like others belonging to the Circassians, cheers

Fig. 22.
View of el-Breikah and Tell el-Akkâsheh.

the eyes of the stranger with its clean and wide straight streets, big hay-cocks, and a well-built

I

mosque. It possesses a spring in the north with icy-
cold water, near which there is a pool, whose water
irrigates the beautifully laid-out gardens of the
Sheikh. The inhabitants are particularly hospitable,
and, thanks to the eminent educated Sheikh, the
chief of the collective Circassian villages, who
welcomes European action and ardently desires
the construction of a railway. The country of el-
Breikeh is stony, but fruitful with splendid pasture
land. In the south also the villages receive some
water from the Seil el-Breikeh and the 'Ain el-
Hajâra. Its position, owing to the Hami Kursi and
Tell el-'Akkâsheh in the west, is very protected and
healthy. As regards antiquities, in the Circassian
villages the settlers have built up and whitewashed,
present but few. It is, however, certain that they
have only settled on the old ruined places where
building stones lie ready to hand, and where
they hoped to find treasure. According to their
testimony, this last hope has not deceived them. So
much as one is able to see, viz., that the old place
was fortified by a strong wall in the east. In the
village itself one finds crosses and lintel ornamentations from ancient times. One of these ornamentations (Fig. 23) is worthy of notice, because on it is
represented the cross and the Jewish candlestick; it
seems, indeed, as if the latter were added as a sup-
plement to the cross.

Breik'ah (C. 8).—A small crumbled ruin on the ·
western declivity of the Wâdy Masâud. A few

Fig. 23.

spendid old trees spring out of the ruins, under
which are some winter huts fallen into decay.

El-Buk'âti (D. 2).—A village of the Druses, consisting of 35 rather proof-built huts, with about 160
inhabitants in Merj el-Buk'âti. This cultivated
district of the Druses has certainly good soil, also
springs and some aqueducts ; but it is cold, and in
winter-time absolutely enveloped in snow. The
Merj is obviously the hollow of a large crater, whose
walls were formed by the Tellul el-Buk'âti, the Tell
esh-Sheikhah, the woody Tell el-Ahmar, and the
Tell Krüm et-Turkoman. An important trading
street, el-Buk'âti, corresponds to the Bokâtha mentioned, but not visited, by Burckhardt. (Ritter,
Erdkunst, p. 162.)

El-Butmîyeh.—Exhibits better masonry than el-
Eshsheh. We also find in the west, near the old
highway, the ruins of an old building called el-Khan,
which contained several apartments 10 feet wide,
divided into two parts by a single arch.

I 2

The arch presents the usual simple Haurân moulding (Fig. 24).

Fig. 24.

Mangers, like those in el-Ahsenîyeh, for the cattle, and a large cistern in the court, testify to the purpose served by the building, namely, an inn.

These remains date from the Arabic age; only the lintels of the entrances, with their Christian symbols—namely, rectilinear crosses, vine-leaf ornamentation, and weather-worn inscriptions—recall an earlier Christian period (Figs. 25, 26). Very peculiar

Figs. 25, 26.

are the greatly weather-worn decorations of a door lintel (Fig. 27), on which may still be distinguished

Fig. 27.

some Greek signs, besides a ten-branched figure. recalling the Jewish candlestick.

The village occupies a position only slightly
elevated above the surrounding country ; it abounds
in old building stones, and possesses a spring with a
large aqueduct in the western neighbourhood.

Dabûra (B. 4).—A winter village of tolerable size,
close to the Wâdy Dabûra, above the Lake of Huleh.
Near the wretched Bedawîn huts a large modern corn
magazine stands. The old site is north of the village,
where a number of very large unhewn building stones
and foundation walls, like in Bêdarûs, are to be met
with. Here also they lie in confused heaps upon one
another. Fine oaks and terebinths grow out of the
once inhabited places. The remains, even at the
present day, proclaim a large, firm, and carefully built
settlement. The position is certainly a peculiarly
fine one, inasmuch as it commands the Lake of
Huleh and its lowlands. On some art-worked fragments I observed a small basaltic column, which
is inserted in the wall of one of the huts deserted in
summer. Near this spot the Wâdy Dabûra has rocky
and steep slopes. It commences at the Tell Abu el-
Khanzîr, and is called at first Wâdy Kefr Naphakh.
At el-'Ulleika the waters of several springs unite in
its bed, and, for the first time, makes below this place
a deep incision into the ground. Just before Dabûra
the brisk stream falls over high basalt walls into a
rounded rock hollow ; it then flows along a narrow
gorge for half a mile and enters the charming plain of

the Lake of Huleh, to which it brings its water near the southern part. The slopes of the Wâdy Dabûra are thickly grown with myrtle (Rîhân and Dôm) ; in the village itself as well as in the neighbourhood there are a great number of liquorice trees (Umm es-Sûs). This ruin, so I have lately heard, is to be again colonized, by the Jews who have settled on the slopes of the Jaulân near Dabûra.

Ed-Dajjajîyeh (C. 7).—Six winter huts, built of old stone, lying on the rear of a hill in Wâdy es-Semakh. They are the property of the 'Arab er-Rekêbât.

Ed-Dann (D. 7).—A stone circle and some small un-hewn building stones scattered about. These, as well as the adjacent lying Rujum el-Fâr, belong to the style of the ancient monuments which have been described under el-Yâkûsa. A second *ed-Dann* (C. 5) is near er-Râwiyeh, in the north-west of Jaulân, and marks one of the Dolmens of that place.

Dannikleh (C. 4).—*See* Khan Bandak.

Ed-Danurîyeh (D. 5). — According to some el-Tanurîyeh, though the former is the official form. It is a winter village with a few huts, mostly decayed, and old building stones, at the foot of the Tell, which is called Umm ed-Danânîr ; the name is derived from Dînâr the old Arabian coin.

Deir 'Azîz (C. 6.)—A small winter village, consist-ing of ten huts on the Wâdy Deir 'Azîz (Wâdy esh-

Shukeiyif). It belongs to the 'Arab ed-Diâb, but is not inhabited in summer.

Deir es-Ba'âh (D. 7).—A hill with scattered ruins and folds in the valley of the Rukkâd, below Kefr el-Ma, with a good spring. The surrounding country is romantically wild. Probably a little castle, for the purpose of plunder, or an isolated cloister, but it is impossible to recognise the design.

Deir er-Râhib (C. 4).—A small ruined village, with important ancient remains south of Nu'arân.

Deir es-Sarâs (C. 4).—A wretched winter village, containing six huts, close to the Wâdy Dabûra. It belongs to the 'Arab en-Ne'arneh, and has few remains.

Ed-Delhamtyeh (D. 4).—A ruin, with a few modern and many old building stones, on the border of the similar named wâdy, which commences between the Tell Abu el-Khanzîr and Tell Abu Yûsef.

Ed-Delweh (D. 3).—A small Bedawîn village, consists of five decayed stone huts in the terribly stony country at the western base of the Tell Abu en-Nedâ. Ruins extend over the hill of the village, and also on the plain. One finds broad rectangular foundations constructed of rude blocks of basalt, destitute of any ornamentation. A good abundant spring rises in the western end of the hill, which irrigates excellent pasture land.

Ed-Dhahr (C. 7).—The ridge, which falls in terraces

from Wely Jâfer at Fîk to Mikiall in Wâdy Fîk. It separates the latter from the Wâdy 'Abûd.

Dhahr el-Ahmar (B. 7).—The narrow ridge connecting the real Kulât el-Husn with the southern mountain range. (*See* under Kulât el-Husn.)

Dhahret Umm 'Assâf (D. 3).—The most easterly hill of the Tellûl el-Mukhfy.

Dibbia (C. 4).—A group of fine trees and insignificant building remains of different ages, and some sheep folds, south-west of er-Ruzanîyeh.

Ed-Dikkeh (B. 5).—This ruin, which is not extensive, but rich in ornamentation, lies close to the Jordan, and immediately north of the Batîhah. Close

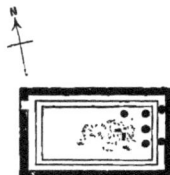

Fig. 28.

Ruin at ed-Dikkeh.

by the stream one sees a decayed mill with an aqueduct, whose construction is far better than that of the mills of modern Jaulân.

The old place stood close by on a small elevation.

One's eye is first struck by a rectilinear building, 55 feet in length and 33 feet in breadth, whose surrounding walls project over the ruins for several feet (Fig. 28). On the north-west corner an entrance leads into the interior, which has two flights of steps 18 inches in height, running all round it. There are traces of good ornamentation on the walls and also on the columns. Between the outer wall and the steps on the east side are two basalt columns standing; they are only 5 feet high. Whilst in the inner room four more of these at irregular intervals tower forth out of the ruin.

Thus the inner was supported by columns. The surrounding walls were 3 feet thick; the building

Fig. 29.

stones throughout have been carefully hewn. Near the two upper column shafts a winged basaltic figure (Fig. 29), cut in bas relief, lies, which, in opposition to

the other ornamentation, lies upon a low artificial
step. The stone is 19 inches long, and 17 inches
broad. Outside the buildings are to be found gable-
like decorations adorned with grapes (Fig. 30), or

Figs. 30—32.

with the Haurân moulding (Fig. 31), beautiful "egg
and pearl" moulding with the native tooth ornamentation, especially ed-Deráah (Haurân), and
several twisted double columns (Fig. 33), also some

Fig 33.

with smooth shafts. The ruins present a Byzantine
character. Nevertheless, if one compare the discoveries in Western Palestine, in the districts of

Safed and Meiron, with those in ed-Dikkeh, a most
striking resemblance between the two appears.
After a searching examination they there appear
evidently as the remains of Jewish synagogues, and,
therefore, perhaps it would not be too audacious to
include ed-Dikkeh among the number of Jewish
buildings (*see* 'Across the Jordan,' p. 243).

Four winter huts of the 'Arab et-Tellawiyeh have
have been erected on the ruined places ; their inhabitants, however, did not present a very friendly face
to archæological research.

Dolmens (B. 4, B. 5, C. 6, E. 6)..—These characteristic remains, of an age of antiquity of which it
is still uncertain, are found in large numbers in
stony Jaulân. Sometimes well, sometimes badly
preserved, in groups, they often cover thousands
of square yards of a district in which the basalt
occurs in slabs. The best preserved is the dolmen
field of 'Ain Dakkar in the upper Zawîyeh esh-
Shurkîyeh of Jaulân, which I have described in detail
in ' Across the Jordan,' p. 62.

It only remains to mention here those places where
they occur, also west of the Rukkâd, and to represent
any especially remarkable shapes.

The dolmen fields of 'Ain Dakkar, called by the
natives Kubûr Beni Israîl, 'graves of the childen of
Israel,' extend in hundreds of well preserved speci-
mens down to the Jisr er-Rukkâd ; they go also west

of this. Single dolmens are to be found north of the bridge as far as 'Ain el-Mu'allakah, where the extremely stony lava region is especially suitable for the necessary material. The dolmens here (Fig. 34)

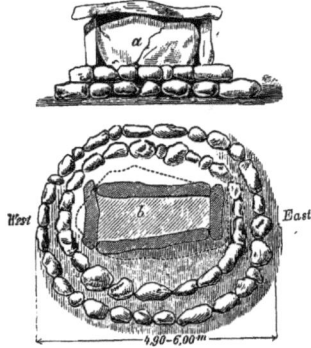

Fig. 34.
Dolmen at Jisr Rukkad.
a. Side View.
b. Plan of.

consist of a double terrace of slabs running from east to west, and which are from 5 to 8 feet in length, 28 inches in height, and 8 to 12 inches in thickness. The narrow sides of the tombs—for these they are without any doubt—are likewise fenced round with a small slab. The rectangular chamber thus formed is covered with a single strong basalt slab, measuring, as a rule, 9 feet long by 6½ feet broad, and 14 inches thick. The west side of the chamber is broader (4½ feet) than the east side (3½ feet); it therefore gets narrower from west to east. This circumstance appears to me to show plainly that we have to do with burial places here; the upper part of the body was laid in the broad western side, so that the face should be turned to the rising sun according to the old practice. The dolmens are elevated on raised terraces from 2 to about 3 feet in height. The floor of the hollowed chamber is covered with earth; on further digging, however, one strikes a rock slab under which nothing was found but the remains of bones and small pieces of charcoal.

In one single place only two rings, 2¾ inches in diameter, came to light; they were made of smooth copper wire ·09 of an inch thick, and had scarcely any perceptible ornamentation.

This was the only find in the way of relics, although several dolmen were thoroughly examined.

On the northern course of the Rukkâd there are very few dolmen; but, on the other hand, they are especially numerous on the western side of the Jaulân, between the Tell esh-Shebân and er-Rawiyeh (see Fig. 35). These, however, are somewhat different

from those found at Jisr er-Rukkâd ; over small
stones, a huge block, 7½ feet high and 6 feet thick,

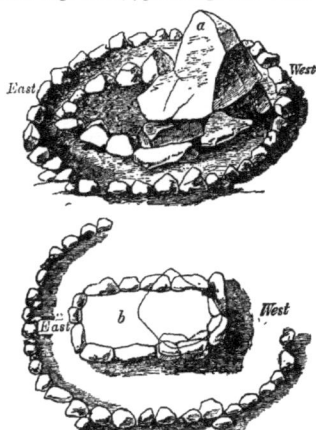

Fig. 35.
Dolmen near er-Râwîyeh (ed-Dann).

a. View.
b. Plan.

formed the roof, for here the basalt is of a somewhat
different formation.

This cromlech is surrounded by a stone circle,

whose diameter is 19½ feet, and 27⅛ inches in height. The western side is open. The chamber has a length of 12 feet, by a breadth of 4½ feet; is not narrowed towards the east, but is facing that direction. The blocks which form the outer stone circle are rudely set; the whole is less skilfully arranged than the dolmen at the Rukkâd.

Proceeding from here towards the south, one finds on the via maris (not far from Nu'arân towards the east) some isolated memorials of this description; and at Dabûra (Fig. 36), near the Sheikh Khalîl, there is a rude circle of large stones, 6 feet high, with a diameter of 33 feet. Over these lie two great blocks, one against the other, having each a length of 8½ feet, by a breadth of 5 feet, and a thickness of 3 feet. The major axis is likewise east and west. The side stones have disappeared, probably broken down under the immense weight. On the slope below Dabûra there are many more similar monuments.

Another extensive Dolmen field stretches from Kubbet el-Karâ to the ruins of el-Kuneitrah. These, however, are all fallen down, and it is very seldom that the top slab is found on the solid substructure. Their construction is exactly the same as those at Jisr er-Rukkâd, only the single constituent parts are smaller. Finally, at Tell el-Muntâr, and on its slopes as far as the ruins Kûsr Bêrdawîl and the Wâdy esh-

Shebîb, we find a large number of dolmen of the same description as those at Jisr er-Rukkâd. These

Fig. 36.
Dolmen at Dabûra.

discoveries are sufficient to show that the Jaulân is very rich in these old monumental constructions. Who made them? When did the giant arm which piled up the enormous block of rockwork live? These questions remain unanswered; but it appears to me certain that these monuments are in any case as old as the original buildings of the Haurân. They must have already come to light in the Roman period, because the Romans appear to have taken care of the Dolmen fields. A comparison between the remains of Roman buildings and these old monuments, which often lie close together, leaves no doubt of the greater antiquity of the latter.

What further induced me to assign their origin to the same time as that of the buildings of the Haurân, the earliest of which are mostly subterranean and roofed with basalt slab, is the striking resemblance which the present Bedawîn tombs bear to the dolmens. They seem to be imitations of those burial places erected by the predecessors of the modern Bedawîn in this country, only the tombs of the latter are much

Fig. 37.
Bedawîn Tomb at Kūlàt el-Husn.

smaller and more insignificant. A characteristic example of such a Bedawîn tomb is found on the Dhahr el-Ahmar of the Kūlât el-Husn (Fig. 37).

K

Two upright standing stones, 23½ inches high, support a small basaltic roofing slab ; the door thus formed is set on the north side in front of the tomb, which consists of rude layers of stones ; a circle of slabs runs round the tomb from each side of the door. On the south side of the stone circle, opposite the door, a remarkably large stone is placed, so that these two points immediately strike the eye of the spectator. The tomb itself is turned towards the south, in accordance with the writing of the Koran that the dead should face the Caaba in peace. This alteration of the position appears, therefore, to have been incumbent upon them from religious motives, whilst the general character of the dolmen has been retained.

Perhaps from other finds we shall succeed in obtaining a more exact insight into that period.

Dôm.—A bramble-bush, with a pleasant tasting sweet kind of hawthorn berry ; it is principally indigenous to the Jordan Valley.

Ed-Dôra (B. 5).—A ruin with eight winter huts of the 'Arab el-Weslyeh, between the Wâdy el-Fakhureh and the Wâdy es-Sanâbir. In the west and south, where the city was not so well protected by nature as in the east, there are basalt terraces of steep incline, and a triply thick wall of great unhewn blocks of basalt. It leads south to a pile of ruins, out of which stems of pillars and Doric capitals, and also a corner pillar, rises. This, I presume, was the old city gate. From here the old city walls run in a sharp angle for a little distance further towards the south-east. On the city gate carefully hewn stones, 6 feet long, are to be found; there are also capitals lying about in other places. In the village itself, which lies inside the city wall, I noticed nothing of interest. A withered 'Fakhireh' stands in the south, which, in spite of its leaflessness, is still always regarded as sacred.

At the foot of the terrace the extremely abundant and fine spring, 'Ain ed-Dôra, issues, and further north-west there is a second one. Both irrigate corn and maize fields and then flow into the Wâdy ed-Dôra, where they turn a mill. This wâdy, like few others, is overgrown with luxurious oleanders and other brushwood, and always contains water, which does not dry up even in the scorching Batihah, at the place called Wâdy es-Saffah, but runs down into the lake.

Between ed-Dôra and Elmîn well-preserved dolmens, with one or two huge top slabs, are to be found.

Ed-Duêr (B. 8).—A ruin close to where the Yarmûk enters the Ghôr. On the river side it is bounded by a steep rock wall, a doubly strong wall, 3 feet thick, built of unhewn stones joined with mortar, protecting it from the accessible part of the plain: this,

K 2

however, is now fallen to the ground, and appears to
have contained only a few large rectangular buildings. One discovers also traces of ruins on the
southern foot of the hill immediately on the Yarmûk.
In the middle of the plateau we find a Bedawîn
stone circle, 16 feet in diameter, the east and west
being marked out by a large stone, having a depression of 5 feet below the surface. There are also
other traces of Bedawîn graves on the slopes of the
hills. Ed-Duêr must certainly have at one time have
served as a point of surveillance for the entrances into
the valley of the Yarmûk, and also as a defence of the
same. The remains appear to belong to the Arabic
time ; probably the place played a prominent *rôle* in
the bloody battle that took place between the
Byzantines and the Moslems, 635 A.D. In the mouth
of the Bedawîn the place is bound up with the name
of the honoured Arabic hero, 'Antar; but I could
not learn any more about him than that he once
lived in Ed-Duêr. They are fond of burying at this
place, and also at 'Abu Kebîr el-Adêseh, a ruin with
winter huts on the southern slopes of the Wâdy es-
Semakh. Traces of an aqueduct, many large hewn
and unhewn old building stones, and some foundations, prove the antiquity of the place. The beautiful
spring irrigates some gardens and a group of palm
trees. The place was not without significance, but the
Bedawîn conceal and cover up in all haste everything

ancient and strange that comes to light for fear of
interference on the part of the Government. It lies
close beneath the rock precipice of the high plateau,
in a wild, uncommonly stony, but richly pastured
district.

Duér el-Lôz (D. 7).—A small pile of ruins in
Wâdy Sîhân.

Duérbân (B. 8).—A shapeless ruin of tolerable size
on the eastern coast of the Lake of Tiberias. It is
divided into two separate heaps, which, however, do
not reveal anything at all as to their antiquity and
purpose. The many building stones are small and
unhewn, and till recently were used to construct
sheep folds. In the time of Burckhardt and Seetzen,
and still later, Duêrbân was a "small village."
(Ritter, ' Erdkunst,' xv., Part I., 267.)

Dûket Kefr 'Akib (C. 2).—Ruins on the coast of the
Sea of Galilee, with scattered building stones, but
few foundations.

El - Ebkuriyeh.—Several sheep-folds, constructed
from the ruins of old buildings. The place must
have once been important, as shown by the many
building stones entirely out of their original position.

In the north the spring of the same name rises ;
its water flows to the spring 'Ain es-Esfera. The
name is not very well known, but it was, however,
guaranteed by the Elders of the village in El-'Al.

It was the same thing with El-Mejdelîyeh, whose position only came to my knowledge accidentally, and
appeared to have disappeared from the memory of
most persons. This ruin, also on the Wâdy
Mu'akkar, does not present anything of interest.

El-Ekseir (C. 2).—A stony district near Skêk.

The neighbouring Merj el-Ekseir is a small, fertile
plain, with an inclined surface.

Elmîn (B. 5).—A large winter village of the 'Arab
el-Weslyeh. The 40 huts are not so badly built as the
other winter villages, but join close to one another,
and form a sheltered, compact house-bulwark, against
the Ghôr wind. Excepting some old building stones,
there are no ruins to be seen. A Moslem saint's
grave, north of the village, with a tree, should also be
mentioned. At the base of the lava terrace, east of
Elmîn, several abundant springs gush out, which
irrigate the dura plants of the beautiful terrace, but
making the ground in parts boggy, render it perilous
for the rider. An uncommonly rich growth of black-
berries spreads over these springs, which constitute
the head-quarters of the Weslyeh. Elmîn lies
immediately over the Jordan, and affords a beautiful
view of it.

Enghtb (B. 7).—A small, miserable village on the east
coast of the Lake of Tiberias, west of Kŭlât el-Husn,
on a low stretch of hills. It comprises 5 huts, with
20 inhabitants. Burckhardt ('Ritter,' 352) calls it

'Um Yeb,' Seetzen 'En Gab,' the correct mode of writing, however, according to the unanimous testimony of officials and Bedawîn, is نفديب out of which comes the vulgar form انفيب.

The Wâdy Fîk, which flows past the foot of the Enghîb-hill, receives here for a short distance the name of Wâdy Enghîb.

Enjâsa (D. 4).—A small ruin, with large foundations of unhewn blocks of basalt in the stony district below Tell Yûsef. The spring 'Ain Enjâsa is feeble. The ruins are so much decomposed that they are only distinguished with difficulty from the fragments of lava lying round.

Esbitteh (D. 5).—A small winter village, belonging to the 'Arab en-Nu'êm, or their branch tribe the Sebârdjah, consisting of 4 huts near one of the highest, most beautiful, and widely seen terebinths of the country.

Beneath the insignificant ruins we notice a cross

Fig. 38.

(Fig. 38), on a door lintel. The place is beautifully situated and high, but has little water.

El-Eshsheh (E. 5).—A small Bedawîn winter village of 20 huts, at the foot of the Tell el-Fâras. It is inhabited by about 80 persons from one year's end to another ; but this place, like the adjoining el-Butmeh, also a winter village of the same size belonging to the 'Arab en-Nu'êm, will soon be entirely deserted, because the Government require this district as pasturage for the horses of the soldiers from Damascus.

El-Fâjer (B. 4).—A ruin, with decayed winter huts, close to the precipitous Wâdy el-Fâjer, which begins near Bôdarûs, in a deep ravine, joins the Wâdy el-Hamd in the plain, and then runs towards the lake of Huleh. In summer it conveys only a little water.

Es-Feiyât (B. 5).—The rugged rock gap through which the Wâdy ed-Difleh flows, breaking through the lava terrace at Suweihiyah. From here onwards the wâdy is called Wâdy es-Feiyât, after this rock.

El-Ferj (D. 5).—A small Bedawin winter village, with decaying huts and old building stones. The Tell el-Ferj, against which the village rests, is supposed to contain a large cavern, but it was not possible for me to investigate this statement.

Fîk (C. 7).—A large village of southern Jaulân, which till recently belonged to the Kada Tubarîya, but as the natives felt themselves thereby injured and in great part deserted it and settled in the environs, it was added to El-Kuneitrah, for which it is adapted by its situation. Fîk, however, is scarcely more flourishing since that time.

Of the 160 existing tolerably well-built stone houses, only about 90 are inhabited, containing scarcely 400 persons, the others are quickly going to ruin (Fig. 39). The place is raised on both sides

of the large Wâdy Fîk or Wâdy el-Kebîr, which commences here to fall over basalt terraces, but soon,

Fig. 39.
The Village of Fîk.

however, becomes broad and pleasing, and in the
bottom of the valley is covered with olive groves.
The view from Fîk down into the valley embraces
first of all the deep-lying Kŭlât el-Husn, and then
the lake, which spreads out deceptively as if it
were lying in the immediate neighbourhood. This
view is very beautiful, but not so open as from Kefr
Hârib. Immediately below the first rock terraces
of the village, the abundant spring, 'Ain Fîk, gushes
forth.

The environs of Fîk are very fertile ; the stoneless high plateau is excellently suited for corn cultivation, but still great tracts lie completely fallow in the immediate neighbourhood of the village. The inhabitants also carry on bee culture.

About 220 yards from the most southern house one comes upon a hill covered with ruins and olive trees, which is marked as a former site by its remains of old columns and building stones.

At the present day the inhabitants of Fîk bury their dead there, and with the object of honoring a Moslem tomb, called the place Jâmat el-'Umeri ; perhaps a mosque stood there at one time. In the neighbourhood there is a second tomb, that of the Sheikh Faiyâd Abd el-Ghani : to each of these saints is entrusted a heap of firewood.

An old graveyard, with a longish hill called El-Mujjenneh, borders these places eastward. The Kusr el-'Ulliyeh lies in the south of the village, on the rising ground commanding the whole neighbourhood (*see* Fig. 39). It is a Moslem building, formerly destined for the reception of strangers, and, judging from the *enceinte* walls, was also fortified. At the time that Fîk, according to the testimony of the natives, formed the central point of the land, Kusr was the seat of Government, the Serai.

Several Ionic basalt and granite capitals of pillars and a quantity of basalt shafts of columns lie round about ; old door lintels, with totally defaced Cufic inscriptions, are situated on the entrances.*

The village possesses an extraordinary number of oil mills, for large olive trees are to be found round this village, as well as on the slopes and in the wâdy. Besides old cisterns, there is a circular well, 25 feet deep, with an edge of hewn stones. In the courtyard of the summer Menzûl of Sheikh Dîab, besides remains of columns, the ornaments of Figs. 40 and 41

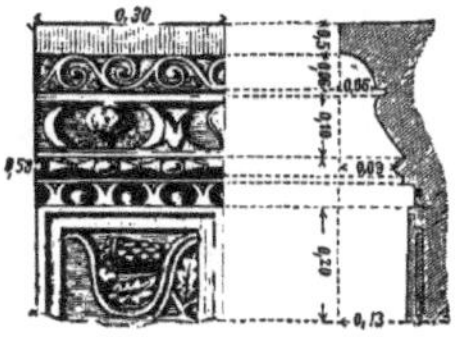

Fig. 40.

Fig. 41.
Ornamentation at el-Fîk.

are found, and in the wall there is a fragment of a

* I took an impression of this inscription, but unfortunately it was destroyed by an involuntary bath in crossing the Jordan. I hope to restore it later.

defaced Arabic inscription* in the year 741 of the
Hegira.

. . . لموا الى الله تعالي الوحيد الدنيا محمد مغبل
. . . ـ احد واربعين وسبع هبات

In the neighbourhood of the Menzûl the more
ancient inscription of Fig. 42 may be observed.

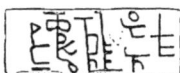

Fig. 42   Fig. 43.
Cufic Inscription.   Greek Inscription.

Further distant, the Greek inscription of Fig. 43
lies on the street. I found the inscription of Fig. 44

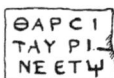

Fig. 44.
Greek Inscription.

* I took an impression of this inscription, but unfortunately
it was destroyed by an involuntary bath in crossing the Jordan.
I hope to restore it later.

over the door of a dwelling-house. Mention must be

Fig. 45.
Column with seven-branched candlestick and Hebrew inscription.

made of the defaced Hebrew signs (Fig. 45), with the seven-branched candle-stick, found on a small basalt column. Another form of this latter is presented on a door post, which has already been given in the Z. D. V. P., viii., p. 333. The constantly repeated ornaments of Figs. 46 and 47

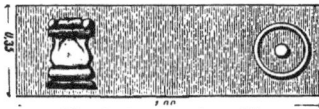

Fig 46. Ornamentation at Fîk.

Fig. 47. Ornamentation at Fîk.

are peculiar to Fîk; equally frequent are the signs, to me enigmatic, represented on Fig. 48.

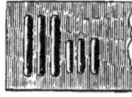

Fig. 48.

Crosses (Fig. 49) are also found on the lintels, and

Fig. 49

the serpent ornamentations of Fig. 50 occur con-

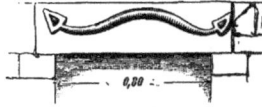

Fig. 50.

stantly ; also the decoration shown by Fig. 51, which

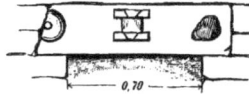

Fig. 51.

Ornamentations at Fîk.

is akin to Fig. 46. Although the figures rendered
only represent a small part of the things still extant,
they are quite enough to prove that Fîk was once an
important as well as an ancient place. As places of
rest for the caravans plying from the Haurân to
western Palestine, they must once have contained a
large market, which, however, has entirely disappeared. According to the statement of the intelligent
Sheikh Diab, the inhabitants of ancient Fîk, in the
middle of this century, built the following villages:—
el-Yâkûsah, Dabbûseh, Jibîn, el-'Al, Skufîyeh (the
youngest), Bîr ej-Jekûm, Kefr el-Mâ, Jamleh 'Abdîn,
and in part Khisfîn. This statement was confirmed
in the villages referred to. Even to-day the dwellers
round ez-Zawiyah regard Fîk as their birth-place, and
tell gladly of the size, wealth, and dominion of the
village. It appears to me to have suffered principally
through the attempt made by Ibrahim Pacha, of
Egypt (1832), to subdue the still somewhat independent Jaulân and Haurân; and also from military
levying and taxation as the former western frontier
place of the Turkish possession. Therefore the inhabitants move onwards towards the interior of the
land, which is only to be reached with great difficulty.
Thus the Porte has completely succeeded in establishing what the Egyptian warrior formerly tried to
do. The Arabic writers mention Fîk; they write it
فيق and افيق, which is unusual in the present

day, whilst the Bedawîn and inhabitants themselves
ronounce it Fij, which points more to a ك‍ than
a ق . One hears not unseldom also Fîka.
Burckhardt calls it ' Feik ' (' Ritter,' 352), and found a
census of 200 families, consequently a much larger
one than to-day. He also gives other interesting
notes about the administration and maintenance
of the place. Of the great Kastel, mentioned by
Eusebius and Hieronymus (' Ritter,' 353), there
is nothing more to be seen, unless the Kusr el-
'Ulliyeh or the Jâm'at el-Umeri fills its place. I
should certainly agree with Ritter and others
that Fîk is the ancient Aphek of the Bible.
(1 Kings xx. 26).

Burckhardt (according to Ritter) considered the
neighbourhood of Fîk was the province of Hippene
(Hippos) ; this assumption would be correct, because,
according to all the old narratives, Hippene lay
opposite to Tiberias, either on or near the lake.
Josephus gives its distance from Tiberias as 30
stadium, 60 from Gadara, and 120 from Scythopolis.
If this statement is correct—which, however, appears
doubtful on comparison with other measures in Josephus, for example, in the description of Tabor (Jewish
Wars, iv. 1-8), Hippos, could only, supposing Gadara
corresponds to the present Umm Keis, be identical
with Semakh or es-Samra. If, however, the statement which I find in Merrill's ' East of the Jordan '

is worthy of consideration, viz., that the Jerusalem
Talmud and other Jewish writings pronounce Susitha
identical with Hippos ; then the extensive although
shapeless ruin Susîyeh, which I discovered between
Kŭlât el-Husn and Fîk, in a plain, elevated half-way
between both, must be regarded as the site of the old
Hippos. I also acquired from the inhabitants of
Kefr Hârib and el-'Al, a rare copper Hippos coin,
which they alleged was found beneath the building
rubbish of this place.

But this alone cannot give sufficient confirmation to
the supposition that the places, Susîyeh and Fîk,
situated between the two spots that have come to
light, belonged to the province of Hippene.

Leaving the village, and turning westwards towards the narrow ridge of the Jebel Zâfarân, we
discover on its northern margin, on the Wâdy Fik,
the foundation stones of an ancient and most solidly
constructed rampart, which extends from the village
to the precipice before Susîyeh ; it probably belongs to that period in which Aphek was called a
' Castell.'

If one descends across this wall and down the first
basalt terrace of the Wâdy Fîk, traces of a walled
aqueduct may be seen which, in spite of the fact that
it is already entirely in pieces and decayed, may be
followed as far as the ruin Susîyeh, and somewhat
further backward.

L

The inhabitants of Fîk assert that in winter time, when the ground is unploughed, it can be traced from Susîyeh downwards as far as the Dhahr el-Ahmâr of the Kŭlât el-Husn ; and upwards through the upper part of the Wâdy Fîk to the Wâdy Abûd, the Jebel Akta Sharîdeh, the Bîr ej-Jêkûm, still further all round the Zawîyeh ej-Jêkûm to el-Awânish, and on the southern margin of the Wâdy es-Semakh to et-Tu'enni, el-'Adêseh, as far as the Wâdy ed-Difleh, where it commences. I myself could not always follow the traces of this aqueduct with certainty ; but Kŭlât el-Husn being an isolated mountain and deficient in spring water, it is very probable that this fort was supplied with water from the abundant Wâdy es-Semakh by means of this canal. In any case, this canal was then as now subterranean, and concealed from the eye of the enemy.

El-Fizâra (D. 4).—A winter village, with about 12 inhabited huts at the foot of the small Tell el-Fizâra. It has some important remains of antiquity.

Fresh el-Lôz (B. 3).—A craggy wâdy, south of er-Rawîyeh, flowing into the Huleh marshes.

Furun (C. 3).—A ruin with some crumbled Bedawîn huts, in an unusually stony region at the western base of the Tell el-Haram. There are several scattered old building stones.

Ghadîr el-Bustan (E. 5).—A ruin on the Rukkâd.

The old weather-beaten building stones lie between
green vegetation, where some springs rise on the river
bed, and in winter form a little cataract on the Rukkâd. A little further up on the Nahr er-Rukkâd, the
exactly similar ruin, Ghadir ej-Jamûs (E. 5), lies ; here
also the remains are insignificant.

Ghadir en-Nuhâs (C. 4).—A shapeless ruin on the
similarly-named wâdy, which builds a waterfall here
in winter. It conveys a great deal of rubble, but
sinks only about 33 feet beneath the rocky lava
plateau.

El-Ghadiriyeh (C. 4).—A small winter village, belonging to the Turkomans. It consists of twelve stone
huts, of which six at most are inhabited, containing
altogether thirty inhabitants. A good spring rushes
along under splendid oak trees, between which some
old masonry is to be found. The Turkomans are
fond of encamping here. These places just mentioned mark the commencement of the Wâdy el-
Ghadiriyeh, which runs into the Wâdy el-Fakhûreh.

El-Ghôr (A. 8).—Only a small part of the Jordan
depression concerns us, viz., that which bounds the
Lake of Tiberias in the south and lies 700 feet below
the level of the Mediterranean Sea.

After its outlet from the Lake the Valley of the
Jordan bears, besides the general name of esh-
Sheriât (a watering-place), the particular name Wâdy
Seisabân, which it retains in the neighbouring district

L 2

of el-Ghôr. It is 3¾ miles broad at the Lake. In
the west the mountains press close on the Jordan,
whilst in the east a fine and most fruitful plain
stretches, which is watered by the Yarmûk ; only the
heat in the valley is so intolerable that it is impossible, even for the ordinary fellahin of Western
Palestine to settle there, and much more so for the
Europeans. It has often been proposed to fetch
negroes from the Soudan and let them cultivate the
ground, which is most productive, and especially
suitable for tropical plant growths, as rice, cotton, &c.,
because these products yield more profit than the sort
of corn, wheat, and barley sown there to-day. The
Dom-bush (*see* p. 130) is a native of the Ghôr. The
inhabitants of the Ghôr belong to the Bedawîn tribe
of the Beni Sakhr ; it is occupied by several branches,
who have cultivated it and made it unsafe.

Hafar (C. 3).—A winter village, consisting of eight
wretched huts on a hill, surrounded by two wâdies,
the larger of which, bearing the same name, forms
the beginning of the Wâdy el-Hamd. Several
unhewn old building stones lie round about.

Hâmi Kursu (E. 4).—One of the highest (3,930 feet)
and most moderate of the volcanoes. A powerful lava
stream flows northward (Tellul Surramân) from the
tolerably destructive crater, opening eastward, and
extends down before el-Kuneitrah. The summit,
Hami Kursu, forms a small stumpy peak, whilst the

Jebel el 'Ayûn

Merj es-Sateh

EL-HAMMEH

Plan of
EL-HAMMEH
BY
GOTTLIEB SCHUMACHER, C.E.
June 1885.

Scale of Yards

slopes, es-Shaáf, fall in terraces, and are cultivated by
the Circassians. A narrow ridge, formerly a crater
wall, runs from the peak to the south-east, and ends
as a cultivated and very fertile plateau, called Rás
Shaáf. The mountain can be ascended on every side
without difficulty; it is overgrown by luxuriant oak
thicket, the remains of an earlier great forest. According to the Bedawin, the summit owes its
designation, Hami Kursu, "Protector of the Crown,"
to the impenetrable oak growth which the Circassians
have for the most part felled.*

In the east and west, as also in the north, rounded
hills lie round the chief mountain.

El-Hammeh (B.C. 8).—The collective name for
the hot springs on the Yarmûk, which rise in the
valley of this latter in a district surrounded by it,
towards the southern part of its semi-circular course,
and bounded on the north by steep rock-walls.

It is under the Kada of the 'Ajlûn, and is valued
by the Bedawin as an asylum which shelters them
from the avenger of blood. If one rides from
Tiberias over the rocky road to el-Hammeh, one
perceives the light-blue pool and the smoking

---

* Compare Wetzstein. 'Das Batänaische Giebelgebirge,'
Leipsig, 1884, p. 14; also in 'Zeitschrift cf. Rirchl, Wissensch.,' 1884,
113. W. writes Hami-Kursuh, and explains it חֹדְבֵּדה קַרְצוֹ
"he who protects bread," *i.e.*, who admits no guest. " Hami-
Kursu" receives its name from its impenetrable wood.

springs from some distance. As soon as one
enters the valley one is surrounded by currents of
air smelling strongly of sulphur. The road leads
through the Rôd el-Bâneh, a waterless wâdy, down
to the Birket ej-Jarab. These hot springs bubble
forth in a natural basin, have a temperature of 104'5°
Fahr., and together have the important outflow of
more than 220 gallons a second. This is soon
collected into a canal, turns a most primitively-con-
structed flour mill, and then flows into the Yarmûk.
Another arm, which carries away the surplus, feeds
a large basin close to the river ; it is 295 feet long,
49 broad, and 8 feet deep ; and surrounded by thick
tree and cane growths, invites one to a pleasant bath.
Then, also, the high temperature of the water has,
by this time, considerably cooled. Quite close to
the Birket ej-Jarab, scarcely 6½ feet distant from it, a
cold spring, 77° Fahr., rises ; it is called 'Ain Bûlus
and flows into the basin filled with hot water—certainly as peculiar a phenomenon as the stream of hot
mineral waters which drives the mill.

The road leads further south, past some palm trees
and remains of ruins, to the principal spring, called
Hammet Selîm, or Birket el-Habel, or Hammet esh-
Sheikh.

It lies 577 feet below the level of the Mediterranean
Sea, has a temperature of 120° Fahr., and an outflow
of 385 gallons a second. At one time a Roman bath

was extended across this spring, as is quite evident from the architectural remains of a large and a small building. The spring bubbles forth in a narrow enclosed basin, deposits, like all the others, a whitish-yellow sulphurous precipitate, which in certain places has hardened into rock-like substances, and conveys its water through several natural-formed basins, which collect and gradually cool it, to the river. Near this spring rises a Moslem burial-place, Wely Selîm, to honour whose saints convalescents and those seeking help plant on the Roman buildings coloured cloths tied to sticks. There also is the principal scene of action of the bathers. The Bedawîn, whose skin is already hardened to leather by the tropical sun of the Ghôr, let themselves down into the smoking, bubbling flood with perfect contentment ; on the other hand, the Arab from the town ventures in first cautiously with the foot or hand, whilst the European prefers to seek out the cooler basin. A little east of the Hammet Selîm lies a small uncovered pool, the Birket or Hammet er-Rîh, which has a temperature of only 93°.2, whilst it makes a similar flow to that of the Hammet Selîm, with whose water it soon unites.

Besides these three principal springs, with their high temperature, nature has also presented this place with good drinking water, furnished by the spring 'Ain es-Sakhneh or 'Ain Sa'âd el-Fâr. This

begins in the north-east corner of the plain as a clear
abundant cold stream, with a flow of 341 gallons a
second.   Fig trees, oleanders, and raspberries grow in
confused masses about the place close below the rock
walls which bound the el-Hammeh on the north.
The stream moves southward through a thicket of
swamp plants, turns a mill, and empties itself into
the river close to the Birket er-Rîh.   A small sidearm
is diverted from the spring westward for irrigating
and filling the troughs for the cattle.   The temperature of this spring is about the same as that of the
'Ain Bûlus, 77° Fahr.   The whole district of el-
Hammeh is covered with luxuriant oleanders and
Dom underwood , it abounds in water, and is consequently somewhat unhealthy, the eastern part being
even swampy, and overgrown with cane jungles.
These springs rise on a flat land of about 1,600 yards
in length, and on an average 550 yards in breadth ;
consequently, on a district of about 180 acres it was
sufficiently large to allow of the erection of a bath
arrangement with all conveniences, as well as beautifully laid-out gardens.   The ground is at present the
property of a citizen of 'Akka, but the springs belong
to the Government.

The western part of the district of el-Hammeh is
rich in ruins.   Near the Birket ej-Jarab an extended
hill rises, on which the remains of a wall are to be
found.   Probably a temple or a castle stood here.

Between this hill and the remains of the Roman bath
there is a strong vaulted building; the floor is thickly

Fig. 52.—Column at el-Hammeh.

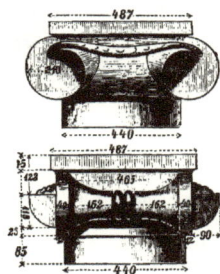

Fig. 53.—Capital at el-Hammeh.

studded with fragments of columns, capitals, bases,
and shafts, and hewn and unhewn building stones. But

it is impossible to distinguish and draw up any plan
of this confused mass. The numerous annual bathing
visitors build huts out of the ruins, or drag the fragments from their places, or dig under the ruins for
treasure; the disorder is consequently always increasing. The upper end of a column and Ionic
capital belonging to these ruins are represented by
Figs. 52 and 53 ; they are well preserved. The ruins
of a Roman theatre (Fig. 54) lie north of Birketer-Rîh.

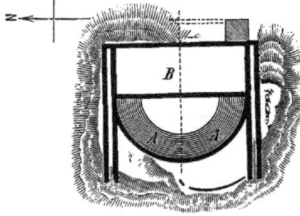

Fig. 54.
Roman Theatre.

The twelve stone tiers of seats (*see* Plan, A) ascend
in an amphitheatre to a height of 19 feet, without a
single corridor traversing them. The seats (Fig. 55) are
18 inches high and 30½ inches broad, and are consequently very comfortable. The uppermost ledge is
formed by a moulding divided into several flat and
narrow friezes (Fig. 56). The diameter of the semi-

circular tiers of seats is only 85½ feet ; the stage,

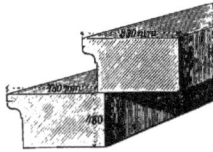

Fig. 55.
Section of Seat.

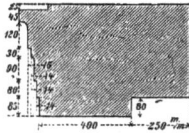

Fig. 56.
Section of Moulding.

somewhat raised by means of the moulding (Figs. 57
and 58), has an equal length and breadth of 33 feet ;

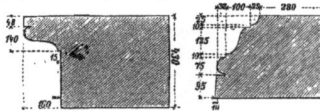

Fig. 57.   Fig. 58.
Sections of Mouldings.

walls 3 feet 3 inches thick, built double on the north and
south sides, surround the whole.   Some dressing and

wardrobe rooms are still attached to the stage place,
but they are almost all levelled to the ground.
Although the theatre is so well preserved that a plan
can be drawn up, the influence of earthquakes is unmistakable, especially on the horizontally displaced
rows of seats. On the convex side of the theatre, in
the west, a hill, 26 feet high, rises, whose uppermost
small plateau spurs show an enclosure wall. The
rock walls which border the district of el-Hammeh in
the north are from 80 to 90 feet high, and fall perpen-
dicularly. A beautiful plain, called es-Sateh, spreads
across down to the foot of the mountain. In these
steep walls, which, according to Dr. Noetling, belong
to a lava stream broken through by the Yarmûk,
several caves open below immediately on the plain of
el-Hammeh; they are not artificial, but are formed
naturally, and are all of insignificant size.

Excavations undertaken there proved that the
upper layer of the ground consisted chiefly of the
dung of the animals that take shelter in these caves,
and that 35 inches beneath the surface a striking
number of remains of bones—of animals first, then also
of men—came to light; they were found to be very
much decayed. Immediately over the layer containing these remains of bones a fine rubbish, with par-
ticles of charcoal, lies. It appears, therefore, that
these caves once served—in grey antiquity, indeed—
as habitations for human creatures.

The caves on the western end of the district of el-Hammeh are of a different kind. Here the lava stream rests on a strong foundation of soft limestone. To the north, above the sharp bend of the river towards the west, distinct traces of human action—namely, masonry—may be observed on the steep caverns, 65 feet high, with walls of lime (Fig 59). As

Fig. 59.
Caves at el-Hammeh.

they are situated from 35 to 38 feet above the rubbish slope of the mountain, they were inaccessible to us. They are already very much defaced. The inner chamber appears to have a tolerable extent. Probably at one time anchorites occupied them, to which the approach may at that time have been more convenient than at present. To-day an examination is only possible if, with the help of a rope ladder, one glides down the channel of the river Rôd el-Bâneh, running close by the caves. Other square apertures are to be seen on the left coast of the river down stream, which, however, are likewise inaccessible without a rope ladder.

El-Hammeh corresponds with the bath Amatha, or the hot springs of Gadara, principally frequented in the time of the Romans. From the hot plain of the springs the bathers have betaken themselves in crowds to the high lying Gadara, or Umm Keis, scarcely half-an-hour's distance, where they can rejoice in the cool air and lovely view. But even to-day, hundreds of natives from all parts of the land hasten to el-Hammeh. Barren Arabian women seek aid in the warm flood, and numerous examples are related of the desired effect of the bath. It is for this reason that one sees especially young women, accompanied by their husbands or relatives; they erect huts of willows and straw, or brushwood; friendly families live close together, whilst solitary strangers seek to protect themselves from the rays of the sun behind the ruins. During the day most of them rest, but as soon as it begins to get dark an animation and deafening noise sets in. To the sound of trumpet and fife, groups of women, watched by their husbands, draw nigh to the baths and divert themselves in the lukewarm pools. They return with the same noise ; and then feasting, laughing, dancing, story-telling goes on in the tent till the early morning, when another bath is taken, and then they retire to rest. And so the visitors to the baths go on for a fortnight or three weeks, whilst the bathing time lasts altogether from April to July. New comers salute those who are there, and are welcomed by them with musket-shots, through which it not unseldom happens that accidents occur, for the sojourners, who are often half mad with excitement, as a rule, fire their muskets close over the heads of those present, and thus frequently wound one or another, as I myself have had opportunities of observing. If the one who is struck belongs to the resident Bedawin, threats are uttered, and stormy events seem likely to come to the fore. Only by a heavy offering of gold from the guilty party to the offended can a bloodless deed be expiated. If, however, blood has been shed the originators hurry off, for the scene of their bloody deed is no longer a sojourn for them. Although every year 100 to 200 tents arrive in el-Hammeh, no conveniences are provided ; they leave everything to mother nature. It would, however, without any doubt, be not only remunerative but also a particularly wholesome undertaking, if the sojourn at these springs were made in a more habitable, pleasant, and comfortable manner. The contents of the springs has been, according to testimony, likened to the Carlsbad water, and already in antiquity, as has been observed by Ritter, 1053, compared with that of Baiae.

Harf (B. 7).—A fair number of scattered old building stones on the Mukatt ej-Jamusìyeh, above Susìyeh.

Háwa (B. 5).—A small ruin with two corn magazines, better built of stone, belonging to the Bedawìn, in the woody district, on the wâdy of the same name, which upwards is called Wâdy ed-Dôra, and lower down Wâdy Jerâba and Wâdy es-Saffah.

El-Háwiyân (B. 8).—A narrow rock gate near ed-Duêr, consisting of two angles of the rock lying opposite each other, which embank into the Yarmûk, the east end of the 'Alâlì ed-Duêr (*see* p. 131).

Hètal (D. 7).—A village on the slopes of a wâdy of the same name, which is somewhat better constructed than the neighbouring Jìbìn, and contains forty stone and clay huts, with about 100 inhabitants. As regards ancient remains, only fragments of columns and hewn stones are to be found. The country and the wâdy are abundantly supplied with water. East of the village on the road is the Bìr et-Trûh, with a pool and oleander bushes. A very primitive tomb has been raised to the wood saint, Sheikh Muhammed; its Mujjenneh protects a quantity of fuel.

El-Hûtîyeh (C. 7).—Four Bedawìn winter huts

above the Wâdy es-Semakh to the south. There is good pasture ground, and some old building stones.

Inkhêli (D. 5).—According to a few trustworthy Bedawin, also called Umm Khêli, is a winter village, consisting of nine huts on the margin of a wâdy of the same name, below el-'Amudîyeh. The remains of ruins are insignificant.

Jamleh (E. 7).—A village of the ez-Zâwiyeh esh-Shurkîyeh, comprising thirty-six dwellings, built of stone and earth, and 160 inhabitants. The village is poor, and has only a little arable land, because the country is stony. But it possesses a few fig-gardens, and some vegetable cultivation. A sufficient quantity of water is yielded by the spring Ain Hamâta, in the south of the village, and by another one in the north. Old remains are scarce, and it is only in the south that we come upon large foundations, with immense blocks of basalt, apparently primeval, as, indeed, everything in Jamleh appears. The view over the ravine of the upper Rukkâd is very beautiful.

Jebâb en Nânâ (C. 3).—A small volcanic hill, overgrown with underwood, east of Skêk.

Jebâta el-Khashab (D. 2).—A large Druse village of Kada Wâdy el-'Ajam.

Jebel 'Ain en-Nhnr (B. 8).—A part of the edge of the plateau south of Kefr Hârib.

Jebel 'Ain es-Sakhneh (B. 7).—A low isolated hill on the plain, lying on the east coast of the Lake of Tiberias.

M

Jebel Aktâ Sharîdeh (C. 7).—The slopes of the plateau, south of Skuflyeh.

Jebel Jûâ (C. 4).—A small pointed hill with a few building remains, near Nuârân.

Jebel Kurein Jerâdeh (B. 7).—The summit of this slope, overlooking the Lake of Tiberias, is 450 feet above the Mediterranean Sea, and 1,132 feet above the level of the Lake, with deeply furrowed valleys. It consists for the most part of limestone (*see* Fig. 20).

Jebel Mokâdlah (B. 7).—A semicircular hill, overlooking the Lake of Tiberias, much broken up by eruptive-rent valleys, probably part of a gliding hill. The warm springs, el-Hammeh (*see* p. 149), spring from its base on the shore.

Jebel Seil el-Aswad (B. 7).—A low rounded hill at the foot of the Kŭlât el-Husn.

Jebel esh-Shârarât (B. 8).—The south-western slope of the Jaulân, between el-Kuweïyir and Khan el-'Akabeh.

Jebel Zâfarân (C. 7).—The narrow mountain ridge between Wâdy Fîk and Wâdy Masâud. On its northern rim there are traces of an old fort wall, extending as far as Fîk.

Ej-Jedeiyeh (C. 6).—A ruin, with some old building stones, close to the Wâdy ed-Difleh.

Ej-Jelébîne (B. 4), written by some el-Klebine. Although the latter form sounds more familiar, I must, after inquiries, recommend the first as being more correct. The place is nearly forgotten, and a desert ruin on the Wâdy Dabûra, near the Lake of Huleh. It has no visible remains of importance, but has the appearance of great antiquity.

Jeraba (B. 5).—A Bedawîn winter village, with insignificant ruins, in the woody country north of the Batîhah. The name recalls the Gabara of Josephus.[*]

Jibîn (D. 7).—A village on the fall of the Wâdy Hetal, which comprises thirty-eight huts of basalt and earth, with ninety-five inhabitants, or twenty-one families, according to the testimony of the Sheikh. West of the village we find the paltry sepulchre of the wood saint, Neby Yûnis, with a small court. North of the miserable village lie the ruins of Jâmât el-'Umeri, a mosque from the time of 'Umeri, at which time the village must have arisen. Besides an ordinary base in the Hâurân style (Fig. 60). there are remains of

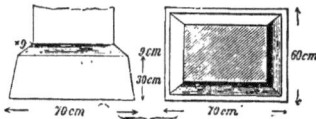

Fig. 60.
Bases of Columns at Jibîn.

---

[*] The Gabara of Josephus (Jewish Wars III. vii. 1. ; Vita 10, 25, 45, 47) lay 40 stadia away from Jotapata ; it cannot therefore be looked for east of the Jordan. Comp. Reland, ' Palastina,' Guérin, Galilee, 771 ; H. Hildersheim, ' Beitrage zur Geographie Palastina's ' (1886), 15, 43.

Koran inscriptions. The outer court of the mosque is overlaid with basalt slabs. The door lintel on the Menzûl of the Sheikh bears likewise a part of the Koran inscription removed here from the mosque ; it is quite defaced, and only the words ــ ـ ـ ـ ـ ـ الله ـ ـ ـ لا are recognisable. Besides olive-presses and quarried stones, there lie the beautiful Attic base of a corner pillar, and a portion of a less well executed Doric capital, with beading on the base. In the village I found an Ionian capital (Fig. 61) and some basaltic

Fig. 61.
Ionic Capital.

shafts of columns, 5 feet long and 14 inches in diameter. The building stones throughout are basalt The village has a superabundance of good drinking water.

The Rân Jîbin (*see* under 'Ain el-Melekeh) is built over the spring, and flows into a sarcophagus.

In the west of the village I discovered several subterranean remains, which are found in such numbers in the Haurân (Fig. 62). These measured only 8 feet square and 6½ feet high. They are walled up, and have a good dressing of ¾ to 1 inch in thickness at the bottom. The covering, which is on a level with the upper surface of the earth, consists of basalt slabs; the layer of wood bushes and clay which lie over it is

Fig. 62.
Underground Chamber.

doubtless a later addition. Whilst they are at present used as corn magazines, they probably served formerly as cisterns, hardly as dwelling-rooms, as a staircase and the necessary openings are wanting. The inhabitants certainly assured me that there were some such with a small flight of steps in the north ; but these, however, are buried under ground.

Jisr er-Rukkâd (E. 6).—Two stone bridges lead across the Rukkâd ; an upper one near Sueiseh, which is therefore called Jisr Sueiseh ; and a lower one, east of Khisfin, called Jisr er-Rukkâd. The first is small, and consists of eight large unequal pointed arches, of

which the three centre measure about 16 feet, the
three on the right side about 15 feet, and the two on

Fig. 63.
Jisr er-Rukkâd.

the left coast side 15½ feet and 10 feet. The height
between the vertex of the arches and the water surface amounts to about 12½ feet in summer. The
bridge is 15 feet broad, and 250 feet long, from one
extremity to the other. The arches are united by
piers 8 feet thick, which have a cuneiform pier-head
up the stream, in order to keep back the rush of
boulders. The pier spaces on both coasts are very
broad. Unfortunately, the bridge is in decay; and
although the quarried basalt stone is built up with
good white mortar, both ends have already fallen in,
so that the approach by a beast of burden is impossible. In winter time only, when the stream has
swollen to an enormous size, they use the footpath,
whilst the caravans have to wait for better weather.

The carriage road of the bridge is entirely horizontally paved with wide basalt slabs. This paving, several miles, is continued on both sides in a Roman road, still well preserved in part, and 9½ feet broad. I conjecture, therefore, that the bridge is also of Roman origin, especially as its design differs from that of the Arabian time, inasmuch as the carriage road does not incline from the centre towards each side, but has a horizontal surface.

Joramâyeh (C. 6).—A ruin near the border of the wâdy of the same name. Till recently it was a winter village of the 'Arab ed-Diâb ; but the huts have fallen to pieces, and it is now deserted. The ruin is tolerably extensive ; the building stones are mostly unhewn and long. One comes upon the remains of subterranean buildings, small rooms with basaltic roofs, like in' Jîbin, which have been transformed into graves by the Bedawîn, and closed up with stone slabs. South of the ruin we find some better modern masonry in a large rectangular room. In the Arabic age, Joramâyeh was still a village of moderate size. At the bottom of the wâdy, below the ruin, some palms flourish ; also, trees grow along the whole length of the wâdy. Wâdy Joramâyeh commences at the western foot of the Tell ell-Fâras, near the 'Ayûn el-Fahm. At first, the brook sinks only suddenly below the surface, then at Tell Bâzûk it suddenly plunges over high rock walls, and forms a

narrow ravine, which widens below the ruins of
el-Kuneitrah ; it is marked throughout by some green
growth. The Wâdy Tell Bâzûk runs in from the
north (*see* p. 129), being only separated from the chief
valley during the last stretch of its course by a
narrow ridge. Both convey their water to the
Batihah, where it soon gets absorbed. The ravine
grows more pleasant, and in the plain itself vanishes
in a flat indent of the ground, marking out the line
of the stream of water, which in winter is very large.

Jort el-Akrá (B. 5).—Close to the east, near a bare
part of an otherwise woody country, with a single
withered tree and some traces of masonry.

Jort el-Hâkîm (D. 4).—A piece of lowland, with a
spring which in winter turns a mill. It is at the foot
of Dhahret Jôrt el-Hâkîm, the rocky eruptive ridge
on the eastern foot of the Tell Abu Yûsef, which is
obviously either a lateral eruption of this crater or else
an old crater wall.

Jort el-Hâwa (D. 3).—The country between el-
Kuneitrah and el-Mansurah. Its name, ' Lowland of
the Wind,' is especially justified in winter, when
through the gap between the sheltering Tell Abu
en-Nedâ and the crater west of el-Mansurah, a cutting
north-west wind sweeps over the plain, causing a
heavy snowfall. Altogether, this is the most windy
tract of country in northern Jaulân. On the other
hand, Jôrt el-Hâwa is a small strip of lowland, be-

tween a strata of lava, near the Wâdy el-Gharâbeh,
above the western slopes of Jaulân.

Ej-Juêtzeh (D. 4).—A large Circassian village of
seventy houses, with sixty families, and 300 inhabitants
collectively. Of antique remains little are to be seen.
Well kept practicable roads lead to the thriving village, which lies in the best pasture country (*see*
'Ain el-Belât for a second ej-Juêizeh, C. 3).

Ej-Jummeizeh (B. 6).—A sycamore (mulberry-tree)
and a Moslem tomb of the Sheikh Rajâl in the
eastern Batîhah.

The tree is of great age and splendid growth.
Some scattered ruins are to be found in the neighbourhood.

El-Kahwâneh (B. 8).—A district of the Ghôr immediately south of the lake between the Jordan and
Tellul es-S'âlib.

Kanef (C. 6).—A Bedawîn winter village east of
the Batîhah, and a magazine of Muhammed S'âid
Pasha of Damascus, occupied by ten to fifteen inhabitants, and is conspicuous from its high position. There
are some old building stones.

Karahta (C. 3).—A Bedawîn winter village, whose
huts are permanently inhabited by from twenty to
thirty persons belonging to the 'Arab el-Hawâj.
There are some tolerably old building stones. In the
south-west there is the Birket Karahta, a dirty pond.

El-Kaseibeh (C. 6).—A Bedawîn winter village of

four huts, with old building stones. It is here that the Wády el-Kaseibeh commences, which further down is called Wády Deir 'Aziz, and Wády esh Shukeiyif.

Kefr Hârib (B. 7).—A village consisting of 70 stone and mud huts with 40 families, or about 200 persons. The inhabitants are affable and hospitable, not like the people of Fik, who are peevish. They have a Khan in the village, the resting-place of the caravans, instead of in Fik. The western side of the village, like Fik, crowns the basalt precipice of the lava plateau in a semicircle, and, as has been already mentioned, affords a matchless view across the country and Lake of Tiberias. Several good and abundant springs break out beneath the first precipice ; they are set in old masonry. The village is not yet old, but is, nevertheless, in a flourishing condition, carrying on an excellent bee industry, and cultivating the stoneless and extraordinarily fruitful plateau stretching south down to the Yarmûk. It is, however, subject to quit rents from a much-esteemed Damascene. In the south the simple monument of Sheikh Muhammed el-'Ajami stands, surrounded by high wood piles and farm implements, and overshadowed by clusters of magnificent trees. In the village itself there are few antiquities, although the old building stones point to large buildings. On the Mahall ej-Jâma'a the smooth ground and enclosure walls of a mosque, with a defaced Arabic inscription, are to be seen ; of this latter I was unable to distinguish anything but عسى الفريز

On a door lintel we came across this not infrequent ornament of Fig. 64, and in the yard of a house the Greek inscription of Fig. 65.

200

Fig. 64.

Ornamented Lintel.

Fig. 65.

Greek Inscription.

The old site south of the present village is marked out by a number of scattered stones, mostly unhewn, with foundations of the Arabic age. Here and again one discovers quadrangular subterranean rooms, very carefully built of hewn stones without mortar ; they have a base area of 6½ by 5 feet, and a depth of 5 feet, and were probably formerly sepulchres ; they are now turned into grain chambers. One of the basalt coverings of these appears to me to have been

adopted later than the remains lying round. After
the old site is passed, we reach broad traces of a wall
which can be followed along the western margin of
the plateau as far as the Sultaneh, stretching down to
Khan el-'Akabeh. Probably they are the remains of
a Roman road, which was bounded by a wall.

Kefr el-Mâ (D. 7).—A large flourishing village on
the Rukkâd with 80 buildings, mostly spacious, of
stone.   According to the testimony of the Sheikh

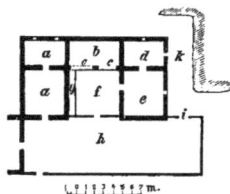

Fig. 66.

Plan of the Sheikh's house in Kefr el-Mâ.

a Family dwelling-place.
b Open court.
c Arch.
d Winter menzul.
e Winter stable.
f Summer menzul.
g Divan.
h Summer yard for the horses.
i Principal door.
k Street.

Muhammed el-Ahsen, who at the present time represents the interests of the ez-Zawîyeh el-Ghurbîyeh
in the Medjlis of el-Kuneitrah, and who is consequently a highly esteemed personage, it is inhabited
by 800 persons. The Sheikh's house in the westerly
part of the village is roomy and well-built. The
Menzûl, which he built, is a two-winged building,
with a large court and open hall adjoining. In the
latter prayers are said during the summer (Fig. 66).
The surroundings are fertile ; the Rukkâd slopes rich
in water. About 82 feet below the village, towards
the Rukkâd, the abundant spring, 'Ain Kefr el-Ma,
gushes from a fissure in the rock. A rounded arch
(Fig. 67) is built over it, above which enormous

Fig. 67.

'Ain Kefr el-Mâ.

basalt rocks tower. Its water falls into a stone
setting, and is conveyed out of it through an old

dyke-channel of black clay to a choked-up ruin lying
near el-Hammeh (bath to the right in Fig. 67).
Here it irrigates some vegetable gardens.

The spring water is remarkably clear and wholesome. In the village itself, the inhabitants of which
practise bee cultivation, there are many ruins to be
found, besides large hewn basalt squares, Corinthian
capitals with acanthus leaf, shafts of columns, and an
entire arched niche with radial shell-like decorations and beading. The real ancient site extends over
a wide field, covered with building stones, west of
the present village. In 1 Macc. v. 26, besides the
Casphor Khisfin, already mentioned, we are also
told of Alema. Now, as the natives of that village
write the name the same way, laying the accent on
the short article before the *l* (Kefrêlma), whilst only
the officials write it Kefr el-Mâ, we are driven to the
supposition as to whether a relic of this ' Alema' does
not remain in the present name. According to the
ordinary form used by the officials, the name signifies
' water village,' obviously with reference to the
richly-watered declivity.

During my stay in Kefr el-Mâ, a fellah quietly told
me that in the yard of his neighbour a Sanam (idol)
had been discovered and again buried. After lengthy
parleyings we came to an agreement to disinter it
by a moonlight night, which we were successful in
doing, to my delight. Fig. 68 represents the statue,

38 inches high, cut in relief out of basalt stone ; it is
a male figure, whose right hand holds a rod up which

Fig. 68.
Statue in Basalt at Kafr el-Mâ.

a snake is winding. The clothing consists of a scaly
shirt of mail which reaches to the knee, and covering the chest. The head is swathed round with a
threefold kind of rope plait. The left arm bears a
broad bangle, and the hand a kind of feathered
arrow. The whole figure stands under a projecting
cornice of basalt stone, and is 3 feet in height, and
19½ inches in breadth, and about 34 inches thick.
It is still found *in situ*, as is proved by the enclosing foundations ; but without further excavation

it is not possible to acquire a plan of the ancient
building.

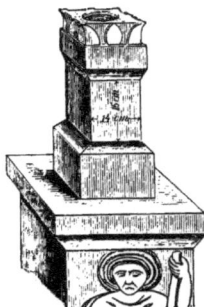

Fig. 69,
Altar at Kefr el-Mâ.

On this block, adorned with the statue, a small
altar stood, which is now to be found in the Menzûl
of the Sheikh (Fig. 69). It is likewise of basalt,
2 feet high, and having a base 9 inches square. In
the centre of its upper surface there is a round cavity
4 inches in diameter. Its ornamentation, like that
of the statue, is tolerably stout and solid, the work
being carefully executed, and apparently very ancient.
I will not venture any suggestion as to the origin of
this statue.

From all the remains found in Kefr el-Mâ and its

neighbourhood, it appears to me certain that the ancient place was once important and rich in architectural buildings.

Kefr Naphâkh (C. 4).—An old Bedawîn village; which has been recently rebuilt by the Turkomans, containing a large well-built corn magazine; old building stones, mostly unhewn and long, appear in large numbers, and, as in the neighbouring Bêdarûs, are heaped up in regular hills, so that one is only able to discover old square foundations with labour.

They are all, however, greatly weather-worn ; the decoration of a large capital can scarcely be any longer perceived, whilst some shafts of columns are also very much injured. In the south of the ruins the Turkomen have hollowed out a well-shaped cavity some yards square, which is bricked in, and about 25 feet deep.

Very interesting are the sliding tombs lying close to the margin of the wâdy (Figs. 70 and 71). They consist of three rows of either thirteen or eleven tombs, the inner of which measures 6½ feet in length, 23 inches in height and breadth. They are separated from one another by basalt slabs, and covered in the same way.

Each row has two layers, one upon another, but all the graves lie beneath the surface of the ground. The rows are divided off by passages 6 feet wide, and shut in from above by a stratum of rock. The

N

main direction of the passages is from north to south.
Towards the south the rocky Wâdy Kefr Naphâkh

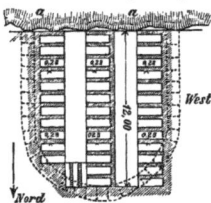

Fig. 70.
Plan of Sliding Tombs.

Fig. 71.
Sketch of Sliding Tombs.

(Fig. 70, *a*), which makes a steep fall of some yards,
bounds the burying-place. The western portion of the
tombs is certainly fallen in, but, all the same, I believe
I have correctly rendered the plan of the whole in
Fig. 70. Not a trace of sarcophagi is to be seen.

Crossing the wâdy we arrive at the Via Maris, and

then to a second ruined place lying opposite Kefr
Naphâkh, with old walls and many building stones.
The region is very stony, but in spite of this, the
earlier place was of importance.   Burckhardt, in
'Ritter,' 168, speaks of a large pool with a circumference of 200 paces, with traces of a stone
aqueduct, which he called Birket Nefah or Tefah,
and which he mistook to be the Lake of Phiala.
The place, according to his description, is identical
with Kefr Naphâkh, but the tank is no longer extant.
Perhaps the long wall running along the southern
margin of the wâdy has been a canal.

Kersa (B. 7).—A ruin on the shore of the Sea of
Tiberias, lying close to the discharge of the Wâdy es-
Semakh. The remains date from two periods ; a more
ancient one, from which only scattered building stones
and foundations are still extant, and a more recent
one, probably Roman, whose long walls, 3 feet thick,
are built of small stones joined with white mortar
similar to those found in Tiberias (*see* note to Kusr
el-Kelbeh). They enclose square rooms.

A round tower, built above the ruin on the lower
ledges of the slopes, dates from the same period.
According to the statements of the Bedawîn, it bears
the name Kersa, or Kursu, because it is not unlike a
stool, whilst the already-mentioned walls on the lake
are called es-Sûr.

Nevertheless, what is usually understood by Kersa is

the ruin generally, which is distinguished by a splendid
Butmeh. The ruins are extended, and it is thought
that traces of aqueducts can be distinguished. The
lime rocks of the neighbourhood have several large
natural cavities, especially over the lower ruin on the
slope. Steep precipices at a slight distance from the
Lake, like Mokaâdlah, and at el-'Arêt ridge of the
Wâdy es-Semakh, are numerous.

Up to now the site has been identified with the
Gergesa * (Matt. viii., 28).

Khalas (B. 7).—Some remains of ruins on one of the
mountain ridges, lying opposite the Kûlât el-Husn.
The slopes down to the foot of el-Kûlâh exhibit
several grave holes cut in the hewn rocks, the passages of which are, however, mostly choked up. I
must postpone for the present a closer investigation of
this place.

Khân el-'Akabeh (B. 8).—A ruined building of the
Moslem period. It was originally an inn for caravans,
and is situated on the principal road leading from
the Jordan to Fik, Khisfîn, and the Haurân. The
Khân has a quadrangular foundation. A yard
for the beasts, measuring 56 feet square, is enclosed
by a vaulted court 16 feet wide, for the reception

---

* The name Gergesa has been introduced into Biblical text
from the reading (νεσηνῶν) Gergasenes in the Gospel of St.
Matthew, which is based on no good authority, but has
obtained currency through the influence of Origen. It would be
well to strike it out. Mark v. 1, Luke viii. 26, &c., refer to Gadara.

of persons. The walls (basaltic) are occasionally
6½ feet thick. In the east a pointed style of gate,
upon which are the remains of a beam arrangement,
leads into the courtyard (Fig. 72). The other pas-

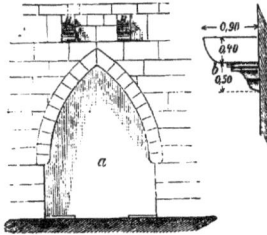

Fig. 72.
Door in Khân el-'Akabeh.
a, front view ; *b*, Section of B.

sages, probably one on each side, are destroyed.
Close to the principal gate in the east there is an
Arabic inscription chiselled in white limestone, but it
is greatly decomposed. An open flight of stone steps
leads from the courtyard to the terrace, which, however, at that time formed a part of the second storey.
The eastern gate, which is 7 feet and 10½ feet high,
is well built of hewn stones. Judging from the pivot
holes, the bar of the gate must have been a very
strong one ; 87 yards north of Khan we find a small
square ruin, no doubt the former watch tower ; 163

yards east is the magnificent spring, 'Ain el-Khân or
'Ain el-'Akabeh, shaded by splendid trees; it flows
south from Khân down towards Tawâfîk. The Khân
is built of huge basalt stones, for the most part
unhewn, between which are to be found some with
raised embossing, 3 feet in size.

This circumstance, in addition to the much weather-
worn, but curiously ornamented basaltic stone in
the courtyard (Fig. 73), point to the conclusion that

Fig 73.
Ornamented Stone in Khân el-'Akabeh.
23½ inches high by 35¼ inches long.

an ancient building stood here, probably dating from
Roman ages. The track of an old highway from the
Ghôr upwards to the neighbourhood of Kefr Hârib
can be followed up; this, however, leaves the Khân
el-'Akabeh lying to the north, and is only connected
therewith by a side road. The highway is edged by
strong squared stone, and served at that time as a
bulwark against the steeply falling off Wâdy, the
edge of which it touches. This ancient highway
generally follows the new Sultâneh el-'Akabeh, down

whose steep descent the caravanserai of the Haurân thread their way all the summer. At the foot of the mountain, where the road crosses the plain Ben et-Tellul, some low round hills lie, which are called Rûs el-'Akabeh (also Rûs Tawâfîk).

Khân Bândak and *Dannikleh* (C. 4) are the names of a Turkoman village. The latter, however, chiefly attaches to a group of fine trees, with some old building remains somewhat south of the village, marking in all probability the ancient site. Khân Bândak contains about forty huts, miserably built out of stone and earth, with 200 inhabitants, exclusively Turkomans, who carry on some field and vegetable cultivation. In the west of the village a spring with a semi-circular enclosure of an ancient period bubbles forth ; its flow irrigates some vegetable gardens. Amongst the ornamentation the seven-branched candlestick of the Jews is represented, as well as the cross of the Christians (Figs. 74–76). The skill manifested in the execution is, however, very inferior.

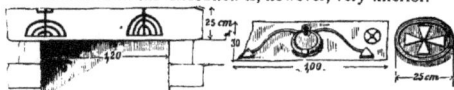

Figs. 74–76.
Ornamentation at Khân Bândak.

The quarried building stones are simply placed in the walls. The space occupied by the old site was not very extended.

Khân el-Barak (B. 7).—A heap of ruins on the declivities north of Kûl'at el-Husn.

Khân Jôkhadâr (E. 5).—A ruined Khân, on the principal highway to Damascus, between Sueiseh and Khisfîn, at the foot of Tell Jôkhadâr. This latter is a hill extending from east to west, the most southerly of the volcanic chain.

Khân esh-Sh'abanîyeh (D. 5).—A ruined Khân in central Jaulân.

Khisfîn (D. 6).—A middling sized village of the Zawîyeh el-Ghurbîyeh. At the time of the Arab supremacy it was an important town, the central point of the district, and even down to the last century was superior to all the other towns of the Zawîyeh. It soon lost its importance and for a long time has been quite deserted. If I remember rightly, Yâkût mentions the town of Khisfîn as a principal military stronghold. Burckhardt ('Ritter Erdk.' xv.) calls it Khastîn, or Chastein, by which designation it is marked in the earlier maps of the Jaulân, and speaks of ' extensive ruins of a city built out of the black basalt blocks of the land with remains of a very important building.' In the history of Judas Maccabeus (1 Macc. v. 26, 36), a city called Casphor, in the land of Gilead, is mentioned near Bosor (Bosra), Alema (Kefr el-Mâ ?), and Karnaim (Tell el-Ash'ary), and which is probably identical with Khisfîn.

To-day Khisfîn, although extensive, is a miserable

village, consisting of scarcely 60 inhabited huts
with a census of about 270 souls.   But three times
as many huts are destroyed and deserted, and good
hewn and unhewn basaltic stones lie in confusion
across one another.   Here and there Roman ornamentation appears (Figs. 77 and 78), and the sign of the

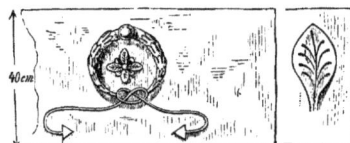

Figs. 77, 78.
Ornamentation at Khisfîn.

cross in a variety of forms on the same stone as shown
on Fig. 119. Most of these, however, are buried beneath
the ruins.   The ruined huts are roofed with basalt
slabs in the style of the Haurân ; several are to be
found beneath the ground.   In the western end of the
city the ruin of a large building is to be found, measuring 133 feet from east to west and 160 feet from
south to north (Fig. 79).   There is a gate entrance
11½ feet wide in the south.

In the west, outer walls, 6½ to 9 feet thick (?), enclose
a passage 19½ feet in width ; then comes an inner wall
only 3 feet in thickness, which surrounds a rectangular
court-yard.   The outer wall makes a kind of oblique

slope and in the east has a buttress ; it is very solidly

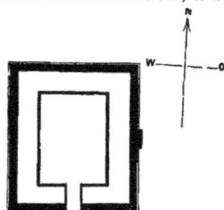

Fig. 79
Ruin in Khisfîn.

built ; the whole gives the impression of a fort or fortified Khan, the architecture of which would probably
be about the time of Yakût, and which, like Khisfîn,
served a military purpose.

El-Khôka (C. 6).—A little winter village with a
few huts, containing about twenty inhabitants. Its
position on the rising high plateau above the Batîhah
is a peculiarly beautiful one.

Khurbet 'Ain el-Hôr (D. 3).—A miserable little village, containing twenty-one huts with about ninety
inhabitants, north of el-Kuneitrah.   Few, or indeed
no remains of any importance, are to be found here.
The spring has a trough, no flow, is in part enclosed
and contains good water.   Every year the village
become smaller, because the inhabitants prefer to
annex themselves to the larger villages.

Khurbet el-'Arâis (C. 7).—' The ruins of the bride,'
lies a little way from the discharge of the Rukkâd into
the Yarmûk, on the steep margin of the high plateau
of southern Jaulân. To-day it is only a heap of ruins
with a strong wall against the incline, which is a few
layers in height and 3 feet thick. Foundation walls
30 feet broad by a length of 13, 22, 25, and even
65 feet, are found ranged upon one another on the
highest places of the ruins, whilst other traces of the
same extend as far as the plain and down the slope.
This was once a settled and important place, as is
shown by its solid construction of large unhewn
basalt blocks set together without mortar. There
are also several bent angled embossments to be
found here. On the slope, about 131 feet below
the ruins, an excellent spring, the 'Ain el-'Arâis,
flows down into the ravine and joins the 'Ain es-
Fejjeh below, which is overgrown with splendid fig
trees, and which trickles down into the Rukkâd.
Beyond Khirbet el-'Arâis a charming undulating
plain stretches right down to the Yarmûk. It bears
the name of the spring es-Fejjeh.

Khurbet el-'Ashek (B. 7).—A ruin close to the shore
of the Lake of Tiberias. It presents several foundation walls about 64 feet square, and lies on a small
artificial elevation. It is probably a decayed Khân of
the Moslem time (Fig. 80).

Khurbet 'Atâr Ghazâl (C. 5).—A small ruin north

of el-Yehûdiyeh, situated on a long extended ridge,
without any particular characteristics.   The 'Ayûn

Fig. 80.

Kh. el-'Ashek.

'Atâr Ghazâl lie on the western base of the ridge.
They have abundant water, and moisten the whole
surrounding country, in which the 'Arab el-Wesîyeh
cultivate some vegetables.   Around the spring are
traces of masonry.

Khurbet el-Batrah (C. 5).—Totally crumbled ruins
of a small village below el-Yehudîyeh.   An abundant
spring, 'Ain el-Batrah, flows in two branches from
the ruins to the Wâdy el-Yehudîyeh.

Khurbet ed-Durdâra (B. 5).—A ruin with scattered
building stones on the Wâdy es-Saffah of the Batîhah.

Khurbet Jiât (D. 3).—A ruin north of el-Kuneitrah.
It occupies a small elevation, and presents a number of
unusually large unhewn basalt stones, the foundations
and walls being 3 feet and more in thickness.   This
place was certainly at one time important and extensive ; the building stones are very much weather-worn
and consequently of great antiquity.   An old highway

set in strong square basalt stones may be followed from el-Kuneitrah to Jiât, where it separates to the north and east. Khurbet Jiât was the first Turkoman settlement in the Jaulân. To-day, with sad faces, they talk of better days, and of the ever-increasing encroachment of the Government and Circassians who have driven them towards the south, and, above all, they regret their robbing trade, which they were formerly able to pursue unhindered. The Merj ej-Jiât, a little plain without any water, stretches east of the Khurbet to the Rukkâd. The Tell Jiât is a small hill on which the ruin leans.

Khurbet Jort ed-Dhahab (B. 8)—A small ruin in the Ghôr on the Yarmûk, at present a Bedawîn graveyard. The tombs bear the *wasm* of the 'Arab Beni Sakhr and the Segur el-Ghôr, and extend over a wide field as far as Abu Kebîr. The environs bear the name of Jort ed-Dhahab to the Tellul es-S'âlib in the north. The (Wâdy) Jort ed-Dhahab is a dry channel in summer, which commences on the plain Bên el-Tellûl, and goes towards the Yarmûk. The entire 'lowland' (Jora) is bounded by the spurs of the Tellul es-S'âlib in the west. This latter is a scarcely perceptible elevation of the ground which the Yarmûk breaks through, and thereby forms the 'Arûk Abu Jedeiyeh.

Khurbet Kôdana (E. 4).—The old site of the present village of Kôdana, north of Tellûl el-Humr. The Khur-

bet is a hill a little south of the village, covered with a
heap of unhewn building stones, which are greatly worn
and therefore of great antiquity.   On its northern base
a lovely running abundant spring rises, 'Ain Kôdana
or Râs 'Ain Kôdana, and which, collecting in a natural
reservoir, forms a watering place for cattle ; it then
flows into the Rukkâd.   Between it and the village a
second but feeble spring trickles from a decidedly
modern enclosure and joins the first mentioned.
At both springs are traces of enclosures and short
aqueducts.   Close by is the village of Kôdana, 6
miserable little huts with 30 inhabitants.   This place,
too, once saw better days, as is proved by the extensive ruins, the carefully hewn building stones, the
remains of rounded apses 9½ to 11 feet wide, from
which, however, it is impossible to draw any plans of
the original foundations, and sarcophagi of basalt
which are sunk into the ground.   The foundation
walls of other old rectangular buildings, without
mortar, are generally 3 feet, and spread over a circular
space.   At the west end of the village there is an
especially large ancient building, called es-Sûr, which
measures 101 feet east to west and 112 from north to
south.   The assertion of the natives that till shortly
before this it served as a Khân is substantiated by the
courtyard for stabling horses which runs round it.
The southern door reminds one of the Haurân style
(Fig. 81), and is apparently the sole remnant of

the original building.   Traces of stone pivots (*a*)
point to an enclosure by means of a stone gate.

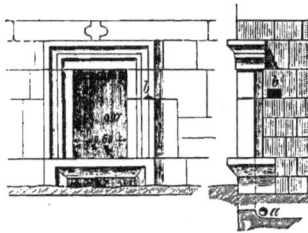

Fig. 81.

Door of es-Sûr.

The keystone of the vertical arch of the door is
very peculiar.

Khurbet el-Médân (B. 7).—A shapeless pile of ruins
on a small plain at the eastern base of the Kŭlât
el-Husn.

Khurbet el-Mudowarah (E. 5).—A small ruined heap
at the foot of Tell el-Faras, lying on the principal road
from Sueiseh to Khisfîn.   It has an excellent spring,
the 'Ain el-Mudowarah, which flows towards the
Rukkâd and irrigates the beautiful country.

Khurbet Mukâtyeh (C. 7).—A few ruins on a large
spring, 'Ain Mukâtyeh, in the plain es-Fejjeh.
The ruins lie close beneath the rock precipices of

Khurbet el'Arâis on the road from Dabbûseh to the Yarmûk.

Khurbet el-Mukhfy (D. 3).—The small scattered building stones of a former village near el-Kuneitrah. On the ridge above this latter lies the grave of the Sheikh Muhammed el-Mukhfy a revered Turkish saint. The tomb is rudely put together out of unhewn stones and surrounded by a plain wall. From him the five hill peaks of the neighbourhood receive the name of Tellul el-Mukhfy. In former times they were so thickly overgrown that one could only reach the sepulchre by great exertions. The remains of woods, thick bushes, and stunted trunks of trees corroborate this assertion. The soil of the Tellûl is of a striking reddish-brown colour, of the same sort as the volcanic cones, and is celebrated for its fertility. Near el-Kuneitrah lies the scanty spring 'Ain el-Mukhfy, with a pool which fills in winter.

Khurbet Sakûkeh (C. 3).—A widely extended but shapeless ruin on the western slope. Sheep folds (Siyar) cover the site ; the building stones are small, unhewn, and devoid of any ornamentation. Very few ruins over so wide a district present such weather-worn building material, with a complete absence of any kind of regular plan. The Wâdy Sakûkeh is small and in summer dry. The name is pronounced by the Bedawin with a softening of the *k*, and also as Sakûjjeh.

Khurbet esh-Shareireh (B. 8).—A small shapeless ruin at the foot of the mountain in the district of Ben et-Tellul. There are no ancient remains, only scattered building stones and a fine spring, 'Ain esh-Shareireh. This rises somewhat higher up, at the foot of the mountain, and irrigates some miserable vegetable gardens.

Khurbet Sîhân (D. 7).—A not unimportant ruin on the wâdy of the same name, which, however, is called above Wâdy el-Khidr. The remains point to two periods of architecture, an ancient and a modern, in which latter the old remains have been used in the erection of small huts.

These, however, are already partly fallen to pieces. Also, this last style of building is not that of the present race, who do not understand how to place the old stones and sashes of doors and windows so carefully and cleverly upon one another as has already been done. The building stones are large, basaltic, and in parts hewn. At present the semi-crumbled places showing traces of basaltic roofing are used as sheep folds. Does not the name commemorate Sihon, King of the Amorites ? At the place where the wâdy begins to sink markedly in the ground, there is a swampy spring on the way with a wide basin called Tiyâh Sîhân, which in winter is full. On the east slope of the Wâdy Sîhân is the Bir el 'Abd, an abundant spring with fig trees, and further down in the

o

wâdy are three moderately large springs, the 'Ayûn Sihân.

El-Khushnîyeh (D. 5).—A large winter village on the Roman street west of er-Rafîd, with scattered building stones. Most of the huts have fallen to pieces.

Kisrîn (C. 5).—A small Bedawîn winter village, with a group of beautiful oak trees and old ruins, south of el-Ahmedîyeh.

Kôm er-Rummân (D. 2).—A small ruin, with the remains of modern huts, cattle folds, and traces of garden plots on the southerly commencement of the Merj el Buk'âti. This place was formerly a Turkoman winter village.

El-Kubbeh, or *Kubbet-el-Karâ* (C. 5).—A Moslem saint's grave, devoid of any art, beneath oaks. Close by is a Bedawîn graveyard, and tolerably well preserved dolmens on the slopes.

The view across the lake, the Batîhah, and the woody district north of it, which is obtained from the Wely, at the summit of the hill, is magnificent.

Kubbet ed-Dhahr (C. 5).—Winter huts of the 'Arab el-Wesîyeh, near some scattered ruins, covering a tolerably wide area.

Kubza Taraiyah (B. 8).—A slope above ed-Duêr, south of Khân el-'Akabeh.

Kŭlât el-Husn (B. 7).—A mountain overlooking the Sea of Galilee, and covered with ruins. It is sur-

Plan of
KŬLÂT EL-HUSN
BY
GOTTLIEB SCHUMACHER. C.E.
June 1885.

Scale of Yards

rounded on the north, south, and north-east by deep
rocky gorges, and as the summit itself is bounded by ,
basalt walls 60 and 70 feet in height, it forms a natural
fortification of a rare description. In the south-east,
only a very narrow ridge, the Dhahr el-Ahmâr, runs
from the summit to the steep ascending Mukatt ej-
Jamusîyeh, falling then also, though at the same time
gradually, to a great depth. This ridge also presents
several fragments of ruins. The plateau is covered
with beautiful oaks and terebinths, which grow out
amidst the rude confused piles of old building stones.
If one throws a glance from the height of Kefr Hârib
to the fortification, the designations el-Husn and
Gamala (supposing that they really lie here), "horse
and camel " (*see*, however, p. 206, note 1), appear
justifiable, for the narrow ridge, Dhahr el-Ahmâr,
clings like a long outstretched neck on to the giant
body of the isolated mountain. Approaching the
Dhahr el-Ahmâr from the Lake through Wâdy ej-
Jamusîyeh, one arrives first at its southern walls.
These embrace the ridge, which is only 90 feet wide ;
in the south, west, and east, having the colossal thickness of 12 feet, and are set in good mortar. The
material used is partly limestone, partly basalt stone,
with bosses which are 5 feet in length, and from 23
to 27 inches in height and breadth. In the west,
where the slopes fall gradually over precipitous basalt
walls, the strength of the walls is diminished, but they

are nevertheless at times built in double. A small
tomb (?) cavern rests against the western wall (*a*). The
eastern wall retains its thickness of nearly 12 feet.
Beyond it large stone heaps may be observed, probably the remnants of two towers (*b* and *c*), the latter
of which measures 25 feet—24 feet encircled by a
separate wall. The many arch stones (?), having the

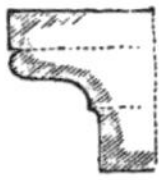

Fig. 82.    Fig. 83.

profile of Fig. 82, half-columns (Fig. 83), fragments of
columns, cornices with egg moulding, prove that an
arched structure stood here. As several sarcophagi
are let into the rock terraces close by in the north,
and likewise outside the wall, this building was probably a mausoleum, as one can hardly imagine a gate
construction here. The sarcophagi, formed of limestone, are from 5 feet to 7 feet in length, 24 inches in
breadth, and 20 inches in height. They are partly
closed by a heavy basalt cover, and then let into a
rock niche (Figs. 84 and 85). Their longitudinal axis
is from north to south. One of these sarcophagi, by
way of exception, is made from 'Ajlûn marble, and

carefully worked with a chisel (?)   On its eastern side
there is, by way of ornament, an arcade with rosettes

Fig. 84.   Fig. 85.

Section of Sarcophagus.

and an inscription tablet. This, however, does not
bear any written characters, but appears to have been
intended for the reception of a metal plinth. The
wreath moulding, that the sarcophagus bears above, is
only a slightly projecting ornament, and seems, like
the rest, to be the work of an unpractised hand ; but
it may be regarded as a leading ornamentation of the
Jewish architectural period at the commencement of
our era. This sarcophagus likewise distinctly extends
from north to south, and is set in a rock niche close
to the northern side of the remains. The northern
end of the cavern-chamber, which is 20 inches deep,
is rounded, forming probably the place for the head
(*see* Figs. 86–90). Proceeding from *c* to 160 feet
further north of the Dhahr, we reach a rock gate (*d*),
that is a gate construction closing one of the passages
cut in the rock, of which only fragments of the bases
(Fig. 91) are remaining.

At this spot the approach to the fort above could be
easily shut off, because the rock walls on each side of

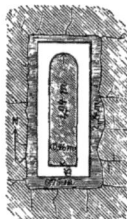

Fig. 86.
Plan of Sarcophagus.

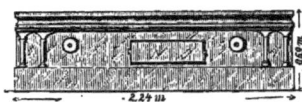

- 2.24 m.

Fig. 87.
Side View.

Fig. 88.
End View.

the gate fall precipitously, and the rock trenches be-

fore the gate would weaken an attack. Behind this
gate there is a Bedawin tomb with a stone circle (*see*
p. 129). The wall in the west gradually vanishes,
but stretches towards the east in a slightly less solid

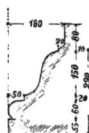

Fig. 89.   Fig. 90.

construction as far as the gate of Kŭlâh, although
the precipitous walls of the Wâdy Shâb Musmâr
afford a natural protection. The slightly rising
ridge has meanwhile contracted to a width of 49 feet.
Over high piled-up basalt blocks which must have
been hurled down from the plateau of Kŭlâh in consequence of an earthquake, the gate of Kŭlâh is
reached, lying 130 feet above the southern extremity
of Dhahr, and 534 feet above the Mediterranean Sea,
or 1,216 feet above the Lake of Tiberias. This gate,
enclosed and protected by huge blocks of rock, has an
original width of 12 feet. Basalt walls laid in crumbling white mortar rise on each side and extend in a
thickness of 13 feet around the margin of the plateau;
they are in part destroyed, and in part preserved to
the height of 3 feet. From the gate, and in the same

breadth (12 feet) a rectilinear street runs which is only once broken, and is paved with basalt flags. It goes over the plateau as far as its western wall, and is bounded on both sides by massive ruins, square foundations, fragments of columns, and defaced profiles. The northern enclosure wall is the weakest ; there the slopes fall at an angle of 36° to 40°, and then as steep basalt walls into the Wâdy Fîk, the wide opening of which was not favourable to an assault or bombardment on this side.

A single tower shows that the gate had surveillance. The southern side has only moderately strong walls, which are in parts 4½ feet thick, but 9½ feet high, and are built over the precipice of the perpendicular basalt rocks with a fall of 65 to 100 feet. A pressure from this side would have been still less to be feared, if the Wâdy ej-Jamusîyeh had not permitted a siege of arrows from the heights of Khalas by means of the narrow aperture it makes here (*see* plan). It is for this reason that two strong towers once overtopped this southern fortification wall. In the west, where the basalt lava runs in terraces, there is a double wall fallen to the ground, with a tower ruin on the southern corner of the wall. Probably also a gate stood here on the western edge of the street, but the ruins are too scattered for any certainty about this. The plateau, or summit, shut in by enclosure walls, hid the city. The visible foundations are

pressed close upon one another ; they are for the most
part hanging together, and in any case only leave
space for a very few side streets in between them. The
length of the plateau, or more correctly the principal
street, amounts to 600 yards ; the breadth varies
between 120 yards in the east, 262 yards in the
centre, and 142 in the west. The building stones are

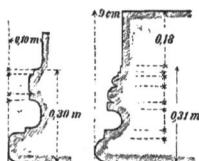

Fig. 91 and 92.
Bases of Columns cut in the rock at Kûlât el-Husn.

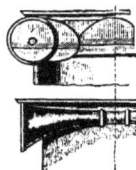

Fig. 93.
Capitals at Kûlât el-Husn.

large and hewn, but much weather-worn ; the capitals

and bases of columns in the Ionic, Corinthian, and
Doric styles show the slightly projecting profile of
the sarcophagus described above (Fig. 86-90).

Very plentiful are the cone-shaped cover ornaments
of columns, which substituted capitals (Fig. 94) : also

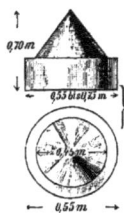

Fig. 94.

Cone ornament.

hollowed shafts of columns (Fig. 95), arch stones of

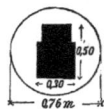

Fig. 95.

the kind shown in Fig. 96, and fragments of pipes,

Fig. 96.
Arch Stone.

probably the remains of an aqueduct, all of basalt
(Fig. 97).

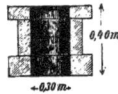

Fig. 97
Section of Pipe of Aqueduct.

The egg ornamentation is absent from the egg-
staved and serrated circlet (Fig. 98); instead only

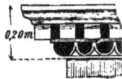

Fig. 98.
Cornice at Kŭlât el-Husn.

cavities are to be seen, which perhaps were inlaid with
precious stones. About the centre of the plateau,
near the principal street, two large still partly preserved buildings stand. The eastern (Fig. 99) is
square, and very strongly walled, its northerly wall
rising on the principal street shows inside a niche

1 m. in width, and was connected by an arch with a
demolished building which adjoins. Near this lies a

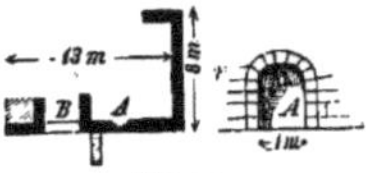

Fig. 99.
Old Building.

granite column 13½ feet long, and 19½ inches in
diameter; others likewise of granite, but only 5 feet
to 6½ feet in length, are to be found in the environs.
Proceeding 100 yards further west, a second building
is met, which is unusually solidly built of great
hewn quarry stones on a rectangular ground plan;
on its eastern side there is a niche 19 feet wide (*see*
the plan, *d*, Fig. 100). Have we a synagogue or a

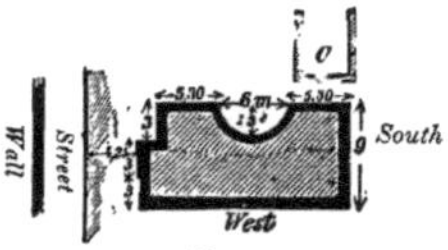

Fig. 100.
El-Habs at Kûlât el-Husn.

Place of Justice before us? The thickness of the
walls cannot be exactly determined. Here also large
granite columns lie round about. East of this niche
there is a large well-filled cistern, 59 feet long, 17¼

broad, and 28¼ high, which is accessible from the east by a flight of steps, and is called by the natives el-Habs 'the prison' (Fig. 100, c). Possibly it was once filled by a conduit. Besides this, there are still several other large cisterns in the west of the plateau. Many depressions and holes in the ground indicate that this city had also subterranean chambers. One of these is still to-day accessible ; it lies close to the northern wall of the western corner of the plateau. A small staircase leads into a choked up, low, but broad room, supported by rafter columns ; its walls are worked in hammer and chisel, but are not dressed. These subterranean chambers probably served as places of refuge during sieges ; there must have also been outlets leading down to secret paths of the mountain, otherwise they would scarcely have constructed these so near the fortification wall where a foot descent is possible.

If we compare Kûl'at el-Husn with the testimony of Josephus about Gamala ('Jewish Wars,' iv. 1.), we can scarcely doubt the identity of these two places. The deep valleys of the sides and front are the Wâdy Fîk and ej-Jamusîyeh ; the transverse ditches are found in front of the rock gate described ; the plateau bore the 'closely' built houses of the city ; the spring inside the wall is the el-Habs which supplied the cistern with spring water by a conduit from without.

As to the subterranean passages and sepulchres

which Josephus mentions, we have probably a trace of
them in the chamber described above in the north-
west corner of the plateau. The old name, Gamala,
which the dwellers did not pronounce correctly in the
time of Josephus,* has been supplanted by Husn,
which signifies 'horse,' as well as 'natural fortification.' As the last meaning is already expressed
by the preceding Kûlâh, we must certainly abide by
the former.

The designation 'horse,' however, recalls the place
Hippos, or the province Hippene, in which, as we saw
on page 195, this fortification must certainly have
laid.†

El-Kuleiâh (E. 5).—A rugged, rocky, crescent-

---

* Josephus says ('Jewish Wars,' iv. 1,) that the natives did
not correctly *express* the exact meaning of the name of this
place (in the pronunciation).

† Compare with this the opinion of Frei in Z. D. V. P. ix.,
130. Frie appears, in my opinion correctly, to reject the
dentification of Kûl'at el-Husn. It is true that some characteristics correspond to the description given by Josephus :
others, however, are so decidedly opposed to the identity that
there is little to be placed on the points of agreement. If one
rigidly compares the statements of Josephus with those given
in Schumacher's carefully sketched plan it is impossible to
resist the impression that Josephus had another site in his mind.
The designation el-Husn cannot be otherwise explained than in
the names Husn el-Akrâd or Kûl'at el-Husn near Homs, Husn
Suleiman in the Lebanon mountains, Husn Hîha north of
Zahleh in the Lebanon district. In all these cases it means
fortification (Socin, Z. D. V. P., iv., 4). The word Husn does
not mean horse, but el-Hisân means stallion.

shaped crater, the most fissured of all the volcanic chain south of Tell el-Faras. In front of the principal western crater lies a smaller and more easterly one, the Tell ed-Dar'aîyeh, probably a portion of an earlier crater.

El-Kuneitrah (1) (D. 6).—A large ruin, with crumbling winter huts on the Wâdy el-Kuneitrah, a side valley of the Wâdy Joramâyeh.

Distinct traces of a city wall run round the square-built place, which stands only a little higher than the plain. The building stones are fitted in white mortar, but are small, and do not recall the finished masonry of the Roman ruins. The foundations also point to large buildings at this place, which belong to the latest architectural style, not counting the most recent, probably of the Moslem era. A dirty spring rises in the north, and flows into the Wâdy el-Kuneitrah.

El-Kuneitrah (2) (D. 3).—The principal place and seat of Government of the Jaulân. The 'city'—so the Kaimakam wishes it designated—consists of 260 buildings, which are mostly well and carefully constructed of basalt stones, and contains, excluding the soldiers and officials, 1,300 inhabitants, principally Circassians. The Serâî is a two-storied and, for this country, fine and solid building ; it embraces a large courtyard, and near the apartments of the officials on the second storey there are dwellings for soldiers and

stables *in parterre.* On both sides of it range evenly
constructed chief streets ; they run from north to
south, are 35 feet broad, and have raised pavements
for the booths of the Damascene merchants.

At right angles to the principal streets side streets
lead to well-built magazines and private dwellings.
It does one's eyes good, after having seen so many
devastated places, to arrive at a flourishing, evenly-
constructed, clean village, whose inhabitants, with
their magistrate, or Kaimakam, an energetic, industrious old Turk, immigrated from the neighbourhood
of the chief Turkish town, have more feeling for
European systems than the citizens of many towns in
this country.

Looking, too, at the towering hay-cocks, the swift,
rattling Circassian carts, the preparation of dried
bricks from the fine earth of the neighbourhood, and,
above all, the cleanliness of the streets, one asks in-
voluntarily, 'Am I in the Jaulân?' The merchants
have for sale pretty nearly all that is required by an
Oriental citizen household. Once, and sometimes
three times, a week caravans bring wares and dried
fruit from Damascus ; here they rest for one day,
crossing the Jisr-Benât el-Yakûb on the following day
in order to reach Western Palestine.

In the place itself turkeys are reared.

The surroundings of this place are lovely and
fertile. It lies on the northern extremity of a high

valley, looks north on the Tellul el-Mukhfy, south on
the Hami Kursu, and west on the great dew and
'rain-distributing' Tell Abu en-Nêda. At an early
hour in the morning a thick fog rises out of its crater,
and envelopes el-Kuneitrah and its neighbourhood in
a damp fertilising mantle, which only subsides before
the rising sun. It is for this reason that el-Kuneitrah
is cool also in summer, but is in winter the scene of a
heavy snowfall, a result of its high position (3,300
feet) and the proximity of the high mountains. We
have already seen that the district is windy (*see* the
Jort el-Hâwa). In the north stands a windmill,
whose naked arms have suffered from the violence of
the storm. Its roof, not having been movable, has
yielded to the strong winds, and is at the present day
useless.

In the middle a splendid clear spring rises, which
yields water in abundance for all. The spring-head
is in a basin 10 feet square and 6 feet deep. It is
called el-Hammâm, and sends off its water in various
directions amidst clayey reeds. One of these, serving
as the flow of the principal stream surrounds the
place in the north, and enters the plain as the Wâdy
el-Kuneitrah. A little further east it feeds some
large natural reservoirs, never absent from any
Circassian village, and then turns slowly to the
Rukkâd. As is obvious from its name, el-Hammâm
was an ancient bath ; the walls consist of hewn and

P

unhewn building stone set in white mortar. Near the
Hammâm rises the modern mosque. It is decorated
with old Byzantine scroll ornamentation, which is
chiselled in peculiarly soft whitish-yellow stone
(clay), and may be considered a masterpiece of its
kind (Fig. 101). Not far from this mosque a beauti-

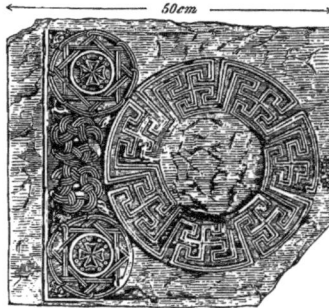

Fig. 101.
Scroll ornamentation.

fully polished granite column stands, 8 feet in length
and 21 inches in diameter, which, at the time of my
visit was brought to the new mosque. Granite is very
rarely met with in the Jaulân, and implies a building of particular importance. Besides the Byzantine
decorations, we find the leaf ornamentation modelled

on basalt of Fig. 102, which is 5 feet in height, and a

Fig. 102.—Leaf ornamentation on Basalt Slab.

characteristic piece of Haurân architecture. On the
door-posts of the Sûk or market one may observe

several crosses on old stones (Fig. 103). Christian

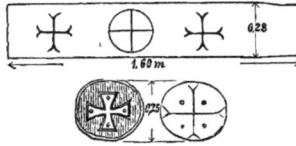

Fig. 103.—Lintel with Crosses.

symbols (Figs. 104 to 106) are also found on basalt

Fig. 104.—Greek Inscription.

Fig 105.—Greek Inscription.

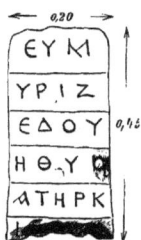

Fig. 106.—Greek Inscription.

tombstones bearing Greek inscriptions in the old

graveyard south of the village, now, unfortunately,
built over. These gravestones are unhewn ; the
inscription is deeply engraved, but with very little
workmanship.

El-Kuneitrah was formerly a Khân, a caravansary
with military stations, at which, as at present, the
camel caravans make a halt, bringing the most
valued articles, such as tea, spices, coffee, dates, &c.,
from Damascus and the valley of the Euphrates.
Twenty years ago it was not yet the seat of Government, and even at the beginning of this century, as is
shown by Burckhardt's Report ('Ritter,' O.S., 167),
was a deserted spot. Burckhardt also discovered
granite pillars on a beautiful mosque, and tried to
identify the old Sik, north of the Khân, with
Kenath. The Khân has disappeared, and the Serâî
arose from its ruins. Very little is to be seen at
present of the old site ; most of the old building
stones have been used again, and only rude, dis-
jointed basalt wall remains are to be found in the
north, not far from the windmill.

The proper building stone of el-Kuneitrah is
basalt. As I have already mentioned, it is made in
part of clay bricks, mixed with fine straw, from
12 by 4 by 3 inches, and then dried in the sun. This
material, made by the Circassian with great care, is
not to be despised, but it does not come up to the
hard basalt, which is so durable.

Kûrm el-Emîr (C. 3).—Vineyards, with a large building near Skek, the property of the 'Arab el-Fadel.

El-Kusbîyeh (C. 5).—Also called el-Kusebîyeh, is a heap of ruins south-west of Selûkîyeh. The highest point is occupied by a totally destroyed square build-ing, on the slopes of which several foundations are to be seen, built of unhewn stones and fitted without mortar. A quantity of building rubbish and stones cover the immediate surroundings. At the western base of the hill a spring set in careful old masonry rises, which is overshadowed by a wild fig tree, and in the abundance, clearness, and purity of its water leaves nothing to be desired. It flows, as an active stream, 437 yards towards south-west, then unites with an equally abundant spring, and after a short course turns a corn mill. They irrigate some vegetable gardens and fields, and finally enter the gorge of the Wâdy Bîr el-Kabak or Wâdy el-Yehudîyeh. The country is stony, but extraordinarily fertile and rich in water.

Kûsr Bêrdawîl (C. 7).—A small ruin close to the fall of the Wâdy ed-Difleh, with several building stones and traces of a large building and choked-up cis-terns. It is said great caverns are to be found in the perpendicular rock walls beneath the ruin. The position of this 'fortress of Baldwin,' who, according to tradition, gladly tarried here, is an imposing one and is naturally protected ; it commands the

deep and broad valley, as well as the surrounding
plateau.

Kûsr el-Kelbeh (B. 8).—' The castle of the bitch.' A
small ruin on a terrace in Ghôr, near the Lake of
Tiberias, 6½ feet in height and 10 feet square. It is
solidly built with white mortar and unhewn stones,
exactly like the Roman ruins near Tiberias; possibly
a small tower or monument. The saying goes that a
company from the neighbouring Semakh had prepared for a journey into the Ghôr, and encamped
here with the object of partaking of a meal. Whilst
the food was being served out, a serpent dashed out
of the brushwood, licked the food, and vanished,
The company fled apart, but soon, however, were
just about to continue their repast when their little
dog snatched a few bites, and immediately sunk
down dead. The food had been poisoned by the
snake, but the little dog had saved the lives of the
party; they therefore determined to erect a memorial.
So narrates the Sheikh of the Arab Segûr el-Ghôr.

El-Kuwetyir (B. 7).—The small sloping plateau of a
hill on the Lake of Tiberias, bounded by steep limestone
rocks ; it has a few remains of masonry on its eastern
half. According to oral testimony, travellers recognise in this place the Gamala of Josephus ; but more
serious consideration should be given as to whether
Kûlât el-Husn is not equivalent to this ancient
place. Moreover, the opinion of the inhabitants that

a ' Burj' stood there once is not improbable, and
agrees with De Bertou's statement ('Ritter,' O.S., 28),
that the rock hill is called ' Khân el-Kueir,' and that
on it is 'a caravansary in ruins.'

El-Láweh (C. 6).—A miserable Bedawîn winter
village and some ruins, surrounded by beautiful oak
trees, on the northern margin of the Wâdy es-
Semakh.

Close by is el-Mushkêrfâweh, likewise a winter
village with a few huts, containing many old building
stones and splendid oaks. Now and then some
Bedawîn families inhabit the huts during the summer. The place is certainly the one which Burckhardt heard named 'Mejeiferah,' near whose ruins
the Wâdy es-Semakh debouched into the Lake, but
which Zeetzen or Bertou found again ('Ritter,' O.S.,
355). The statement about its position is, on the
whole, not incorrect, because el-Mushkêrfâweh lies
above the debouch on the plateau.

For the pronunciation of the name, see index.

El-Maghrîk (C. 1).—A small flanking plain of the
Merj el-Yafûreh, not far from Mejdel esh-Shems, so
called because the melting snow inundates the seeds
and smothers them.

Several water-trenches soak through it.

Makâm el-Emîr (C. 2).—The tomb of an old Emir
of the 'Arab el-Fadel, lying north-west of Skek, and
overshadowed by a group of magnificent trees.

Makhâd Esbêh (C. 5).—A passage of the Wâdy Ghadir en-Nuhâs, near the rock gate Shâfât Esbêh.

Makhâdet el-'Adêsîyeh (B. 8).—A ford of the Yarmûk at Abu Kebîr.

Makhâdet el-Ikful (B. 8).—A ford on the Yarmûk, near Khurbet Jort ed-Dhahab.

Makhâdet el-Mar'eiyeh and *Makhâdet Umm esh-Sherûb* (C. 8).—Two fords of the Yarmûk below and above Makhâdet Umm Kharrubeh.

Makhâdet es-Siyarah (B. 5).—A ford of the Jordan, at a rapid part of the river, between the Lake of Huleh and the Lake of Tiberias.

Makhâdet Umm Kharrubeh (C. 8).—A ford of the Yarmûk below Dabbûseh.

Makran el-Widiân (B. 6).—This is the name of the swampy delta formed in the Batîhah by the debouching of the rivers into the Lake of Tiberias.

Mamid el-Ma'ânik (B. 8).—A long extended ridge of the slope at Khân el-'Akabeh.

El-Mansûrah (D. 3).—A large Circassian village, near el-Kuneitrah, comprising about 90 villages and 400 inhabitants. It is growing rapidly, and shares with el-Kuneitrah and Ayûn es-Suwân the splendid plain, stretching between the two volcanic ranges, for its agriculture.

El-Mansûrah (D. 5).—A small Bedawîn winter village on the upper Wâdy Joramâyeh, containing only four huts, without any ruins worthy of notice.

El-Medjàmià (C. 5).—A heap of ruins, the stones
mostly rough and unhewn, and decaying Bedawîn
huts in a beautiful position at the commencement of the
woody district north of Batîhah. A good spring rises
550 yards further north. The neighbouring Wâdy el-
Medjâmià (Wâdy, ed-Dalieh), only 25 feet deep here,
has clear, vigorous-flowing, good water, and countless
fish in the rock clefts. Riding from here to the large
ruin el-'Aselîyeh, one crosses a splendid wood district
of terebinths, oaks, and wild almond bushes, within
which small tracts have been made arable, and where
the good stoneless basalt soil ought to be productive.
This region forms a depression, or more correctly the
last terrace of the lava torrent, which falls from the
high plateau to the Batîhah, and is spread over with
an alluvial layer sufficient for agricultural purposes.
Traces of old roads and nameless ruin heaps are very
plentiful in this beautiful district, which seems to
have been created for a small colony. Water, like
building stones, is very plentiful, and if this portion
of the Batîhah could be subjected to systematic
cultivation, a highly rich agricultural district, measuring over 8,000 hectares, would be enclosed.

If these were also to take place in the ez-Zawîyeh
el-Ghurbîyeh in the south-east, then a high plateau in
a central position, with an area of at least 1,500
square miles, would be accessible to human labour,
producing the most important fruits, and which

would not be too far distant from Palestine and its sea coast.

This district would border on the east, the magnificent Haurân, with its extended corn-fields and towards north-west, lie near the upper Jaulân, with its luxuriant pasturage for cattle breeding. A single railway line would place this district in communication with the central point of our civilisation.

El-Medjnûneh (C. 8).—One of the characteristic smooth terraces of the Yarmûk declivity, similar to the plain es-Sateh (roof) near el-Hammeh.

El-Mejdellyeh (D. 6).—(*See* under el-Ebkûriyeh.)

Merj et-Tabel (D. 2).—An undulating district south of Jebâtâ el-Khâshâb, in close proximity to which a sacred tree stands.

Merj el-Y'afûreh (D. 2).—A plain south of Mejdel esh-Shems, flooded by the Nahr es-Sa'âr, which latter turns some mills, and irrigates the poplar groves (Hôr) and meadows. The plain is named from the whitewashed cupola of a Moslem saint, which is situated in the southern part of Birket Râm ; the water of a rich spring flows by it, and turns a mill in the neighbourhood of the Birket Râm.

El-Mes'adi (C. 2).—A hamlet consisting of 60 huts, deserted in summer, near the Birket Râm, belonging to the adjoining Mejdel esh-Shems.

The inhabitants only use the huts during seed and harvest time. Every door is fastened by a block of

wood or piled-up stones, but the huts themselves are
carelessly built.

El-Mes'adîyeh (B. 6).—A ruin and winter village of
the 'Arab el-Tellawîyeh, on an artificial elevation of
the Batîhah on the Lake of Tiberias.

The ruins, with a few palms and fruit trees, the
last remains of a once large vegetation, are unimportant, although extensive ; the building stones are
mostly unhewn. The place is surrounded by marshes,
and consequently unhealthy.

The Wâdy el-Mes'adîyeh or Wâdy es-Saffah, debouches west of the Wâdy ed-Dalieh, and east of the
ruins, into the Lake. To me it appears that the old
site corresponds to the Biblical Bethsaida Julias,
because, at the present time, it lies quite close to the
Lake, and in earlier times must have lain immediately on the Lake (*see*, however, under et-Tell).

El-Mezra'a (C. 2).—The village opposite the winter
quarters of the Fellahîn, is on the Wâdy Za'ôra.
In seed time it is used for storing grain. In summer,
i.e., from May to the end of July, the Mezra'a is
deserted, like the winter villages of the Bedawîn.

Mikiall (C. 7).—A ruin without importance in
Wâdy Fîk with some pools grown round with olive
groves.

Môbarah (D. 7).—Extremely rocky and wild slopes
on the northern bank of the Rukkâd, near Kefr el-Mâ.
Some remains of ruins and caves are to be found in

the basalt rocks bounding the plateau; they are called Tâket el-Harîreh.

Môbarat 'Ayûn (B. 8).—A district close to the precipice of the Wâdy 'Ayûn, north of the same-named ruin.

El-Mudowarah (C. 7).—A ruin and some winter huts on the small plateau of Lime-hill, on the upper Wâdy es-Semakh.

El-Muêsi (C. 3).—A small pile of ruins at the foot of the Shâfât Küttah. Near it stands the Shejert el-Muêsi, an isolated tree with a few ruins. The district is a solid mass of lava, and uncommonly stony.

Mukatt ej-Jamustyeh (B. 7).—A terraced slope above Külât el-Husn. (*See* p. 195.)

Munesêh (D. 4).—Two newly-established Circassian villages, one of which leans directly on the northern promontory of the Hâmi Kursu, and contains 22 huts, whilst the other lies somewhat more west on the plain, and consists of about 60 buildings. Both flourish more rapidly than the other Circassian villages, are well and spaciously built, and have together a population of about 330 persons; there are few old building stones.

El-Mûriyeh (E. 6).—Heaps of ruins and sheep-folds on the steep fall of the Nahr er-Rukkâd.

El-Mushbak (C. 6).—A heap of ruins at the spot where the Wâdy esh-Shebîb and the Wâdy ed-Difleh join the Wâdy es-Semakh. Great basalt building stones and some splendid terebinths mark out the place. Still more ancient building remains and a luxuriant plant growth are to be found towards the east.

El-Mushkĕrfâweh (C. 6).—(*See* el-Lawíyeh.)

Nâb (D. 7).—Ruins on a hill in the ez-Zawíyeh el-Ghurbíyeh district, with the spring 'Ain Nâb in the north-east, and an old stone enclosed pool in the south-west, which is partly fed by the spring.

Beneath the debris lie large unhewn and hewn stones, basalt columns, and the usual Haurân ornaments, very much defaced. The walls of the fallen-in old buildings are 29½ inches in thickness, and arranged in courses as shown by Fig. 107.

Fig. 107.
Plan showing layer of stones in wall.

Burckhardt speaks of a rain-pool—Nam—in this district, which is probably identical with Nâb.

Nahr er-Rukkâd and *Nahr es-Sa'âr* (D.F.E.).—(*See* pp. 31, 33.)

Nakasa (B. 7).—An extended but shapeless ruin on Jebel Zafârân, near Fik, distinguished by its beautiful situation.

Namrah (C. 2).—A small ruin, with crumbled winter

huts and sheep-folds, and a few old building stones, near the Birket Ram.

Nu'arân (C. 4).—A large ruin on the via maris. Here the roads part, the via maris taking a more northerly direction to el-Kuneitrah, whilst the second (es-Sultaneh) strikes east over er-Ruzanîyeh to the Tell el-Faras. According to native tradition, in earlier times Nu'arân was an important caravan station. The ruins are on a hill, whose rocky eastern part falls into a valley watered by a spring. They indicate two kinds of construction : a subterranean, to which rooms covered with basalt flags belong ; and to a Roman, from which the walls jointed in mortar and column ornamentation date. In the north there are walls from 31 to 35 inches thick, which are in courses like those in Bêdarûs. South of the ruin a building, called el-Hammân (Fig. 108), rises 10 feet above a good spring amongst fig trees and palma christi bushes. The edifice is laid in mortar, and has a fallen-in cupola in the east, and an antechamber in the west. The walls are about 3 feet thick ; the cupola was built of small stones, with a good deal of mortar, &c., and is of the same description as the Roman remains in Tiberias.[*] Steps lead up from the spring to the building, which in former times was probably a bath. On a stone near a cross (Fig. 109, *a*) is to be found several ornamentations which appear to have been only scratched with

[*] Compare my note to Kusr el-Kelbeh on p. 216.

an iron graving tool, for instance, an eagle (Fig. 109, *b*),
which, like the other ornaments, is defaced, and only
exhibits a small measure of art. The decorated stones
have rounded upper edges, are long and narrow, and
must have been used as brackets or corbels. On the
building stones of the northern part there is a kind of

Fig. 108.—Old Building in Nuârân.

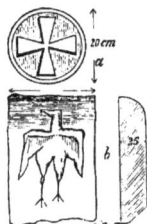

Fig. 109.—Ornamentation on Stones.

rosette decoration. The capitals, Fig. 110, *a* and *b*, are
basaltic, and in the Doric or Haurân style.

Q

Burckhardt speaks of the ruins of a town, Nowarân, which, in Crusading times (Wilken, 'Gesch der Kr.,' ii.,

Fig. 110.

Capitals in Nuârân.

68, according to Ritter), was called Nuara. According to Schubert's observation, walnut and oak trees grew near the abundant springs, but to-day we only find fig trees and palma christi shrubs.

Er-Rafîd (E. 5).—A considerable ruin on the principal highway, near Tell el-Faras. Although the huts of the Bedawin are destroyed, these still encamp in the immediate neighbourhood, and seek for treasure in the old ruins. In the middle of the ruins is an old aqueduct, which conveys the water from a spring which rises in the north of the plain. It is called 'Ain er-Rafîd, and is celebrated for its abundance and excellence. An eastern arm flows into the Rukkâd. The district abounds in water as well as pasturage, and recently been seized by the Government. Two periods of architecture are distinguishable in the ruins. The old Haurân style below, and the Arabian one above ground. To the former belong small subterranean remains, overlaid with basalt slabs, which are rudely constructed ; there are also a quantity of unhewn basalt blocks. Portions of buildings originating in the Arabic period are found on the surface of the ground ; they are better built, and separated into two parts by an arch.

The arches bear Haurân characters, as in el-Butmîyeh (Fig. 111). Their apartments contain in parts stone

Fig. 111.

cells (*see* Fig. 112). The square doors present over the lintel square apertures 20 inches square, executed in the Haurân style, or instead of that a rosette, 10

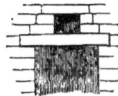

Fig. 112.

Door in er-Rafîd.

inches in diameter, similar to the centre one (Fig. 113). The subterranean walls, as well as those above ground, are as much as 3 feet in thickness. To the Christian period belong the carefully hewn door posts which are partly decorated with a rectilinear cross, and partly in the manner of Fig. 103. The ornament of Fig. 114 is more peculiar. In the south-east of the

Q 2

Fig. 113.   Fig. 114.
Ornamented Lintels.

place we find traces of foundations of a building with
apses, probably of a church (Fig. 115). Some of the

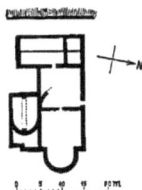

Fig. 115
Plan of Church?

stones are large and carefully hewn, some are rude.
The wall course, about 3 feet thick, follows without
mortar, and in such a way that the stones of the single
courses, which are 12 to 16 inches high, lie across
each other diagonally in the manner shown on
Fig. 116.

Fig. 116.
Sketch showing Stones in Wall.

Beneath the ruins several vaulting and keystones

lie, proving the construction of a dome-shaped apse. The outer sides of the walls appear to have consisted throughout of carefully hewn stones.

Er-Rafîd, so far as the quantity of building stones and the well-preserved parts of buildings are concerned, is one of the most important ruins in the Jaulân, and must have been inhabited till quite recently. Altogether, antiquity seems to have early recognised the value of the fruitful irrigated district between el-Kuleï'ah, and the Tellul el-Humr, Tell el-Faras, and the Rukkâd, and to have adorned it with solid structures.

Rakâkiyah (C. 8).—The lava terrace bounding the Yarmuk below Dabbûseh, an eastern flank of the plain es-Sateh, near el-Hammeh ; the 'Arak Rakâkiya are the slopes of the plateau overtopping this terrace.

Râs el-Hâl (E. 7).—Also called Tell el-Ehdêb. A pointed hill on the eastern slope of the Rukkâd, which probably had its origin in a gliding hill, and which bears some ruins on its ridge (*see* p. 35).

Râs esh-Sheikha (B. 8).—A mountain prominence near the Khirbet esh-Shareireh, north of Khân el-'Akabeh.

Rasm el-Hîrân (E. 5).—A rocky ridge, the termination of a lava torrent, with some ruins, east of er-Rafîd, on the Rukkâd.

Er-Râwiyeh (C. 3).—Eleven winter huts belonging to the 'Arab el-Hawâj, with some old remains, under which are foundations, and in the west a large enclosing wall, built of rude basalt blocks. Beyond this a square cavity in the ground is likewise set in old masonry ; the last is perhaps an old reservoir. In the neighbourhood there are several dolmens.

Rod el-Bâneh (B. 8).—An arid wâdy, which debouches from the north into the Yarmûk, near el-Hammeh. (Comp. p. 158.)

Er-Ruhtneh (E. 4).—A small Circassian village, north of el-Breikah, with about 40 houses and 180 inhabitants. The village has only just originated, but is regularly constructed in a fertile irrigated region, near the Rukkâd.

Rujum el-'Abdeh (B. 6).—A small volcanic hill, with some ruins and fig trees in the Batîhah. The copious spring, 'Ain Musmâr, rises at its northern base.

Rujum el-'Abhar (C 7,.—A large heap of ruins of weather-worn building stones, covered with 'Abhar or lilac.

Burckhardt also mentions it, as it lies on the road from Fik to Khisfin.

Rujum Abu Mashâk (C. 4).—The leaf-stripped hill near Nu'ârân, so called because till a few years ago an oak visible to the whole district stood here, which was felled by a sacrilegious hand. Some old building stones lie near.

Rujum el-Butm (C. 7).—A small hill of ruins, with

sheepfolds, consisting of old building stones, not far
from el-Yâkûsah.

Rujum el-Fâr (D. 7).—An ancient and ruined pile of
rude basalt blocks on the Rukkâd, forming the eastern
limit of the district of Fîk.

Rujum el-Khiyâr (C. 7).—An ancient memorial
(*see* p. 270), composed of rude basalt blocks.

Er-Rumsanîyeh (D. 4).—A large ruin on the ridge
and slopes of a hill. A quantity of large unhewn and
hewn stones tower one upon another in such great piles
that a plan is not possible. In the west we find a
somewhat isolated building, with circular apses in the
north, shut in south by square foundation walls. A
little nearer the hill, more subterranean chambers are
discovered, roofed with basalt slabs 6 feet long, which
contain crypts like those in Kôdana ; near and above
them are shapeless piles of building stones, probably of
the Roman period. On the northern summit of the extended volcanic ridge, running from north to south, rises
a large, ancient, but newly-restored building, whose
plan is illustrated on Fig 117. A large chamber,
divided by pointed arches, 9 feet high, strikes a
smaller one from an opposite direction. The arches
are 27 inches, the enclosing walls 35 inches in thickness. The building stones used are throughout
carefully hewn. At the head, certain bits of discon-
nected walled-in masonry tell us that the building
was erected in Moslem times from the ruins of the

Christian buildings. This assumption is supported on the one side by the existence of pointed arches, on

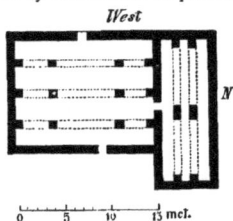

Fig. 117.
Ancient Building Restored.

the other by the description of ornaments found on the old fragments. The first ornaments which strike the eye, coming from the west, are to be seen over a door the lintel of which bears three characteristic crosses, with grapes, and the letters M. and N.* (Fig. 118).

Fig. 118.   Fig. 119.

Ornamentation on Lintels

The lintel on a door to the east (Fig. 119) has two crosses, and between them a defaced ornament. On

* It is probable that A. should be read in place of N., and hat M. stands upside down. Thus "Alpha and Omega."

the ground near the door first-mentioned lies another
ornamented lintel of basalt, with a Greek inscription
(Fig. 120).

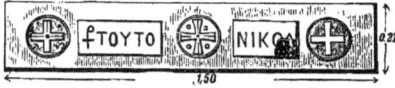

Fig. 120.

Lintel Stone with ornamental Crosses and Greek Inscriptions.

Inside the building one sees close to an arch stone a
large cross (Fig. 121). On another the festooned

Fig. 121.

Cross Ornament at er-Rumsanîyeh.

ornamentation of Fig. 122, and more remote, placed

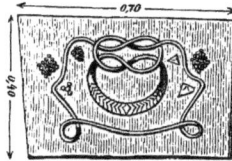

Fig. 122.

Ornamentation on Stone.

indeed on the top, the ornamentation of the arch

stones, Fig. 123 and Fig. 124, with palm trees and
rosettes.

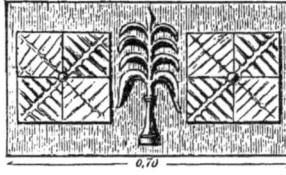

Fig. 123.

Ornament at er-Rumsanîyeh.

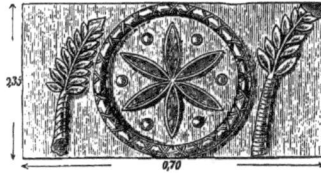

Fig. 124.

Ornament at er-Rumsanîyeh.

Another arch stone, likewise placed on the top,
bears the Greek inscription of Fig. 125 round a palm
tree.

Besides which the walls are covered with festooned

ornamentations of the same description as that shown
in Fig. 122 ; these, however, are more or less greatly
defaced. So that here there must have been a greater

Fig. 125.
Greek Inscription at er-Rumsanîyeh.

development of art than at any other place in the
Jaulân, with the exception of Fîk. The present
building is still overlaid with basalt slabs and corbels,
similar to those in the building mentioned under
Jibin.

Towards the east, at the base of the precipitous
hill, there is a natural pool of spring water, the Birket
er-Rumsanîyeh, whilst in the west the 'Ain er-Rumsanîyeh dispenses abundant and excellent water.

The ruins stretch to these waters, so that they have
a considerable extent. Interesting as they are, their
exact purpose has hitherto remained uncertain.

Er-Ruzanîyeh (C. 4).—A wintervillage, belonging to
the Turkomen, with huts of stone and earth. Only a

few antique remains of building stones are to be found. An abundant spring, the 'Ain er-Ruzanîyeh, rises in the east. The wâdy, named after the place, is here less deep, craggy, and rent. It begins near ed-Delhamiyeh, and is called at first after this name; it conveys but little water, and below er-Ruzanîyeh takes successively the names—Wâdy Ghadir, en-Nuhâs, Wâdy ez-Zawâtîn, and Wâdy ed-Dalieh. It is the most important watercourse of the Batîhah. The principal road across the Haurân to er-Rafîd touches the place, which in former times must have been important.

Saffûreh (C. 7, 8).—A crumbled winter village, the better huts of which are inhabited by from two to six persons. There is some woody and arable land in the surrounding country, but few old remains.

Sahel el-'Arrâbeh (B. 8).—A region on the margin of the plateau on the extreme southern tongue of the Zâwîyeh el-Ghurbîyeh, with a group of magnificent terebinths. The district of Sheffet Mobarah touches it on the east, and extends as far as the ruin 'Ayûn.

Es-Sanâbir (B. 4).—A ruin with 15 winter huts, between the similarly named wâdy and the Wâdy el-Fakhûreh. The remains of antiquity are unimportant.

Seil el-Ghôr (D. 7).—A dry wâdy at Kefr el-Ma, whose upper part is also called Wâdy Muâkkar.

Seil el-Hejaf (D. 4).—A small stream, which rises

near the Jerkessen village, ej-Jueizeh, and flows past
er-Rumsaniyeh into the Wâdy el-Bîreh, where, however, it soon dries up. At its discharge into the
Wâdy el-Yehudiyeh it is called Seil el-Kurdiyeh, a
rocky and deep river bed.

Selûkîyeh (D.4).—A ruin on the same named wâdy,
not far from a spring also similarly named, situated
on a small hill with a number of large unhewn building
stones. The ancient remains, spreading over a large
area, appear literally to have been made level with
the ground, for it is only at the highest point that
one can perhaps distinguish the foundations of a
large square building and some smaller ones. On
the southern bank of the wâdy extended remains are
also to be found. At the present day only cattle-
folds rise out of the ruins. Although without any
further evidence than that presented by the affinity
of names, I nevertheless believe to have found again
the old Selucia, built during the dominion of the
Selenkiden, according to Josephus ('Jewish Wars,'
ii., 20), a fortified city on the border of Agrippa's
kingdom. It is true that the place of modern
Selûkiyeh does not exactly correspond with the
statement of Josephus, that Seleucia lay on the Lake
Semechonitis, whereas in fact by its position the
place is naturally protected.[*] ('Jewish Wars,' ii., 20.)

* The present Selûkîyeh has been already mentioned by
Dr. Thomson, 'The Land and the Book' (1883).

Semakh (B. 8).—A large village on the southern bay of the Lake of Tiberias, containing 65 huts, which are mostly built out of clay-bricks made from the rich soil of the Ghôr to be found at this spot, and afterwards dried in the sun. The bank of the Lake rises here by way of exception to a height of 38 feet, and makes a steep fall. The 330 inhabitants are mostly immigrants from Algiers ; they speak some French, and are very affable ; one also meets negroes from the Soudan. The village, like the country round the Ghôr, is the property of the Sultan ; it is thereby exempt from taxation, and under a governor, and, consequently, in a much better condition than the neighbouring places. The inhabitants cultivate the tobacco plant, and grow vegetables on a large scale. Water is yielded by the Lake. In the Menzûl of the Sheikh there are several basalt columns, about 36 inches in length and 12 inches in diameter, which have been used as props for the rooms. Otherwise the village, which is lacking in building stone, has few antiquities. Burckhardt wrongly regarded the country as Tarichea ('Ritter,' o. 345, seq.). At that time the village consisted of 40 basalt and clay huts, and was governed by a subdued Beni Sakhr Sheikh ; later travellers took it for Hippos.

Serâi (D. 7).—A ruin on a hill near Kefr el-Mâ. A large number of old building stones lie piled on one another, and only a few walls of a modern village are still standing upright. At the foot of the hill, which rises 25 feet above the ground, a spring rises, surrounded by oleanders, whose water flows down over rock terraces into the Wâdy Serâî, which bounds the ruin in the south. On the western slope of this wâdy, under a beautiful tree, the Shejeret el-'Ajameh, the tomb of a Moslem saint, lies.

Esh Sha'âf (E. 4) is the name given to the entire range of the Hami Kursu, although this last name only designates one peak. Some large well-preserved dolmens are to be found on the Râs esh-Sha'âf, the most northern height. The slopes are cultivated in terraces by the Circassian, and thereby the luxuriant oak thickets are entirely done away with.

Esh-Shâfeh (D. 7).—The region between Hetal and Khurbet Sihân, on the bank of the Rukkâd.

Shâfet Kutta (C. D. 3).—The lava torrent of the Abu en-Nedâ and Tell el-'Urâm, a frightfully stony chain of hills, overgrown with oak underwood.

Shâfet es-Sindiâneh (E. 4, 5).—Two hills between the Tell el-Faras and the Tell el-'Akkâsheh. A dense oak wood must have once stood at the place of the oak underwood.

Sheffet esh el-Ghorâb (C. .D. 7).—The fall of the plateau by Khirbet el-'Arais. Many ravens (Ghurab) still fly about and nest in the basalt rocks as in olden times.

Sheffet Tabak el-Melâweh (D. 7).—A region between Khirbet el-'Arais and Jibîn.

Esh Sheikh Khalîl (B. 4).—A Moslem saint's grave, over-shadowed by a terebinth and an oak. Near by are the large dolmens already described (*see* p. 123), of which there are several similar ones in this district, especially on the slopes towards the Lake of Huleh.

Shejeret el-'Ameri (not *'Umeri*) (D. 6).—A tree with a Moslem tomb in the Zawîyeh.

Shejeret el-Musterâh (C. 6).—An isolated tree, on a road beyond the Wâdy es-Semakh, under which the native travellers are accustomed to rest.

Shejeret Matallat el-Bahrein (C. 3).—Some trees, in stony Jaulân, near Bêdarûs, which are well known to the natives on account of the outlook over both Lakes in the Jordan valley.

Shejeret Umm Eshsheh (C. 2).—A large fine tere-binth, near Skêk. In the environs of Ard Shejeret Umm Eshsheh there are traces of an old road, with large basalt blocks on each side.

Shertât el-Menâdireh (7, 8).—(*See* p. 38.)

Esh-Shomarîyeh (C. 4).—A lowland and a wâdy, with a spring near Nuârân.

Esh-Shukeiyif (C. 6).—A small Bedawîn village on the wâdy of the same name, containing only a few old remains. In its upper course the wâdy is narrow and rocky, but, in its lower, broad, pleasant and cultivated.

Shuweikeh (C. 4).—A ruin and a few decayed Bedawîn huts, the old site of el-Ahmêdîyeh (p. 70).

Es-Sindiâneh (C. 4).—A winter village of ten huts, in the midst of a beautiful woody country, with some old building stones.

Sirb el-Butm (B. 8).—A district of the plateau above the Khân el-'Akabeh.

Sirbet el-Kharârîb (B. 8).—A district of the plateau south of Kefr Hârib.

Sitt Iskêne (B. 7).—A destroyed hut on the northern slope of the Wâdy Fîk, near Kŭlât el-Husn.

Siyar el-'Arbâtu (D. 5).—A large number of cattle folds on the Wâdy Bêdârus. The same designation for folds is repeated near the ruins of el-Kuneitrah.

Siyar er-Rashâd (C. 7).—Folds for the Bedawîn pasturing, near Fîk, during the winter.

Skêk (C. 2).—An important ruin, covering an area of about 30 acres, and a winter village of the 'Arab el-Fadel. In the north one meets with a modern crumbled building, which was probably a Khân, as Skêk is situated on a principal road. Inside its walls the Bedawîn have built huts. The place has many cisterns, which are partly filled with water and partly choked up, and a number of large old building stones, with foundations from ancient and modern times. A pool (birkeh) is found in the east, beneath the high-lying place, and in the north lies the Jôbet Skêk, formerly a large tank cut in the lava rocks.

R

Skûfiyeh (C. 7).—A large flourishing village on a
raised point in the western Zawiyeh, which affords a
magnificent view over the lake and the plateau. It comprises 70 huts, which are built partly of mud and
partly of stone, and 350 inhabitants. The village
divides into an eastern and a western portion, con-
forming to the nature of the humpy hill on which it
is built. The neighbourhood is fruitful, but somewhat
lacking in water. In the east we find artificially cut
caves, measuring 13 feet square which are approached
by steps, and arranged as straw magazines ; the walls
are, however, totally blackened. Near the graveyard, in the south of the village, there are some old
stony foundations of a rectangular building, which is
called el-Kŭlâh, and several choked-up cisterns. On
some stones, rectilinear crosses in relief are to be
found ; and in the back stoves and rooms of the village
a striking number of copper and, to me, unfamiliar
defaced inscriptions, the casts of which were unfortunately lost in the Jordan, but will be set up again.

Sueiseh (F. 4, 5).—A village on the Rukkâd, from
which the bridge across the Rukkâd already mentioned
gets its name. It is reckoned with Jedur, and was not
visited by me. It is said to have been bestowed upon
el-Maghârbeh, Sultan of Morocco, by the Turkish
Sultan, as hereditary and private property.

Summâka (C. 3).—A winter village of the 'Arab el-
Fadel, consisting of 20 huts, with some trees and old

building stones on a small hill. The circumference of the old site is tolerably large. Some have found in this the place from which the Huleh lake has received its name, 'Semechonitis,' from Josephus ; but the distance of this place from the Lake is too great for this assumption to gain approval. Rather might 'Semechonitis' be reconciled with the name of the springs on the northern foot of the Tell esh-Shebân, viz., 'Ain es-Semakh.*

Surramân (D. 3).—Three large Circassian villages, containing together about 200 buildings, and 900 inhabitants. Near the two south ones there is a large tank and old masonry. The antiquities have almost entirely disappeared, that is to say, they have been used in the walls of the buildings, and whitewashed. According to the positive statements of the natives, who were acquainted with the ground before the existence of the villages, this was covered with the remains of a very ancient extended site.

---

* The above comparison is found, for example, in Dr. Thomson's 'The Land and the Book,' 1883. The last consonant in Summâka is obviously not favourable to it. The tracing back of Σημ χωνῖτις, Σεμεχωνῖτις to the Arabic Semakh (fish) is already noticed by Reland, 'Palestine' 262, where also other explanations are to be found. The fact that the Arabic plant named Summâk is sounded by us Sumakh cannot come into consideration here at all. The Arabic Summak is σούμαχ σουμάχι ; Italian, Sommaco ; Spanish, Zumaque ; French, Sumac. Comp. Low, 'Aramäische Pflanzennamen' (1881); see V. Hehn, ' Kultiarpflanzen und Hausthiere.'

R 2

The Bedawîn called it Surr el-Mâl (Secret of the Treasure). It was this name, so the officials of el-Kuneitrah assert, that drew the Circassians hither, who, indeed, have actually discovered several valuable finds, which partly explains the large colony and swift rise of the villages. However, to divert attention from their property, the Circassians have turned the name into Surramân.

Sûsiyeh (B. C. 7).—An extensive but completely indistinguishable ruin, on a small plain east of the Kûlât el-Husn. Plough and hoe have worked among the old building stones, and obliterated all remains of ancient days. In the north, a crescent-shaped ridge, the Serj Sûsiyeh, which has probably slipped down from the southern slopes over the ruins, stretches along to the Wâdy Fîk. It also bears some ruins. Sûsiyeh is probably identical with the Susitha of the Jerusalem Talmud (Merrill, ' East of the Jordan '), and consequently with Hippos.*

It lies about 1,115 feet above the Lake of Tiberias, over which one gets an open view from Serj Sûsiyeh.

Es-Sûwâneh (C. 2, 3).—A stony region near Skêk.

Suweihîyah (B. 5).—A few winter huts of the Arab el-Weslyeh, with scattered old building stones lying about.

Tâhûnet el-Ulleikah (C. 8).—A mill of the most

* With regard to Susitha, comp. ' Newbauer Géogr. du Talmud,' p. 238, seq. ; Furrer, in Z. D. V. P., ii. 73 b.

primitive description, on an island in the bed of the Yarmûk, to which a part of the water power of the stream is conveyed by means of an aqueduct built in mortar. A second fallen-in mill lies somewhat more north-east, in the Wâdy Keleit. At this place the river bed is covered with extraordinarily luxuriant cane jungle.

Tât Ahsein (C. 4).—The name of a spring in stony Jaulân, on the via maris.

Tawâfik (B. 8).—A small ruin below the Khân el-'Akabeh. The small unhewn building stones lie in heaps on a hill. It is from this ruin that the projection, Râs Tawâfik, lying south-west, receives its name.

Télestân (C. 3).— An inhabited Turkoman village, with 20 huts well built of stone and 100 inhabitants. The name is probably Persian, and undoubtedly marks an old site, near which traces of old roads are to be found.

Et-Tell (B. 6).—A large winter village of 'Arab et-Tellawîyeh, who take their name from this ruin. It contains 60 carelessly built huts on the north-west margin of the Batîhah. These huts, with extremely few antique remnants, cover the south-west slope of a small hill, past the foot of which the spring, 'Ain Mûsmâr flows, turning a mill at the Jordan. From ten to fifteen persons from et-Tell have built huts round this latter, which they inhabit permanently;

they have also laid out some gardens. At the foot
of et-Tell, on the spring 'Ain Mûsmâr, stands the
tomb of the Sheikh 'Abdallah ; it is surrounded by
a great stone circle and overshadowed by bramble
bushes. East of et-Tell rises a volcanic hill, between
which a small wâdy stretches.

Et-Tell has been frequently connected with Beth-
saida-Julias by Seetzen, Smith, and others.

But this place appears to me to be too far inland
for a fishing village, being 1¼ miles distant from the
Lake. From this point of view el-Mes'adiyeh has
manifestly more recommendations. Besides which,
up to the present, there have not by any means been
more ornaments or inscriptions discovered in et-Tell
which would lead to conclusions as to the past of this
place than in el-Mes'adiyeh. In one respect only, et-
Tell favours the widely spread assumption, viz., in its
elevated position commanding the plain. Is it not
possible that el-'Araj marks the fishing village, et-Tell,
on the other hand the princely residence, and that
both places were closely united by the beautiful roads
still visible ?

In this case, if the industry of earlier days had
disappeared in the former, the glory and the
splendour of the seat of the Tetrarchs would have
given way to a heap of wretched huts.

Tell Abu el-Ghêtâr (D. 7).—A lengthy volcanic hill,
extending from north to south, on the western bank

of the Rukkâd. Broad steps lead up to its most eastern point. Above lie large shapeless stones of ruins which appear to have been ranged in a crescent round the upper end of the steps. The ruins extend on every side over several acres of the land, nearly up to Kefr el-Mâ. The Tell was probably either a watch tower or an ancient place of worship. From here to the Tell edh-Dhahab, which is about 1 mile, and covered with ruins, the whole district is strewn with scattered building stones, out of which, however, no coherent plan can be recognised, especially as the surrounding country is an unusually stony lava region. The Tell edh-Dhahab is an old site.

Tell Abu ej-Jaj (C. 3).—A small lava hill west of the Tell Abu en-Nedâ.

Tell Abu Katif (D. 4).—An isolated hill near the Circassian village ej-Jueizeh.

Tell Abu el-Khânzîr (D. 4).—(*See* under Tell Abu Yûsef.)

Tell Abu Kubeis (E. 4).—A small lava hill between Kôdana and the Rukkâd.

Tell Abu en-Nedâ (D. 3).—' The dew-endowed hill,'[*]

---

[*] Abu en-Nedâ is not the name of the mountain, but the name of the saint who is worshipped on the hill. This is proved without any doubt by the following names lower down of Wely and Makam Abu en-Neda. See also as regards this height of Jaulân, Wetzstein, ' Das Batanaische Giebelgebirge' (1884) 15, and for Tell Abu en-Neda in particular, the remarks of Wetzstein's in ' Delitzsch Jesaia,' p. 707.

the largest volcano in the Jaulân. Its highest point
rises 4,132 feet above the Mediterranean Sea and 721
feet above the high plateau bordering it. The partially
destroyed crater-belt slopes from south to north, and
has a circumference of 3 miles, of which the upper
crater opening has a width of 1,148 yards from east
to west, and a length of 1,331 yards from north to
south. The crater hollow is cultivated by the
Circassians and is very fruitful. Many volcanic cones
lie therein. The mouth of the crater is 612 feet
deeper than the highest point of the mountain. The
inner slopes of the crater fall in an angle of 34°
towards the horizon ; and the slopes of the mountain generally in an angle of 22°. Powerful burnt-
away fragments of lava project over the crater-belt,
falling below 40° or 32° towards the horizon, eastward,
(Fig. 126). On several basalt fragments, which have

Fig. 126.

Crater of Tell Abu en-Nedâ.

been used as Bedawin tombs, the leaf impression is
clearly to be seen (Fig. 127). The western and
eastern longitudinal walls of the crater have an

exactly parallel profile.* The highest point of the
Tell takes in the large well, or Makam Abu en-
Nedâ. This is 38 feet long, 21 feet broad, 8 feet

Fig. 127.

high, and has two whitewashed cupolas which can
be seen in the whole country. The sepulchre of
the great Moslem saint lies enveloped in silken
cloth in the southern division of the building.

In the afternoon the view from this Makam is
magnificent, but in the morning thick misty clouds
arise from the crater and obscure the whole country
till 10 o'clock in the morning. The people, therefore,
view the height of the Tell with gratefulness, as it
yields them, they believe, the fertilising dew. If it
ceases, the destructive east wind is approaching.
Constant violent winds push down the tree growth
on the heights, which first develops into a fine oak
wood at the southern foot. The ground covered

* With this compare my survey of the Tell Abu en-Nedâ in
Dr. Noetling's 'Geologischer Abhandling uber den Dscholan.'

by the Tell is of a yellow colour. The lava streams
of the Tell pour forth westwards ; remains of them
are to be found there in the Shâfet Kutta, and a
frightfully stony lacerated district.

In the south is the small fore-lying volcanic hill,
Abu Rumêt.

There is also a curious piece of antiquity to be
found on the roof of the Wely Abu en-Nedâ, viz.,
the peculiar image, 2 feet 3 inches high, of a bird,
which is fashioned in basalt, and reminds one of
Egyptian or Persian art (Fig. 128). Unfortunately
the head is wanting.

Fig. 128.

Closely connected with the Abu en-Nedâ is the
Tell in the north, called el-'Urâm, 'heaps of wheat,'
on account of its shape, whose slopes strike the

lowest portion of the crater-belt of the Abu en-Nedâ. Its great oval crater opens more to the west, and is as characteristic as that of the Tell el-Faras. Its belt is still fairly preserved, and reaches a height of 4,042 feet above the Mediterranean Sea, and is consequently only a little lower than that of the Tell Abu en-Nedâ. Its lava torrent appears to unite with that of its neighbour in the Shâfet Kutta. Its lowest western slopes are overgrown with oak underwood (*see* Fig. 129).

Fig. 129.
Tell Abu en-Nedâ and Tell el-Urâm, from Kh. 'Ain el-Hôr.

Tell Abu Yûsef (D. 4).—A tolerably well preserved volcano lying south of Tell Abu en-Nedâ, 3,375 feet above sea-level, with an oval crater opening westward. An old crater wall, the Dhahret Jort el-Hâkim lies in front of it eastward.

The double hump-backed Tell Abu el-Khanzîr is less expanded and more destroyed ; its height is 3,819 feet (above sea-level). The lava streams of both craters are apparently confluent at ed-Delhamîyeh.

A splendid oak wood stands at the western foot of the Abu Khanzîr.

Tell Abu Zeitûneh (D. 7).—A hill with the grave of a Moslem saint beside a tree, north-west of Kefr el-Mâ. In earlier days it must have been planted with olives, to which the old mill-stones lying about testify. Many scattered old building stones are found between the Tell and the place Nâb, up to Khisfîn.

Tell el-Ahmar (C. 2).—The most imposing of the mountains enclosing the Merj el-Buk'âti.* Its peak (4,060 feet) rests on a broad base, and its slopes are thickly grown with oak underwood. Its lava torrent falls in regular terraces from the top to the west and north.

Tell el-'Akkâsheh (E.4).—A volcano with a destroyed crater opening to the west. The slopes are overgrown with oak underwood, and the highest summit (3,480 feet above sea level) with splendid oaks, which overshadow the tomb of the much-esteemed Nebi el-'Akkasheh, a nominal brother-in-law of Muhammed. The Wely has a cupola on a superstructure 15 feet

* With regard to the second half of this name, Schumacher wavers between the forms el-Buk'âti and el-Bukâ'ti. Wetzstein, 'Das Batanaische Giebelgebirge,' s. 15, writes it 'Tell Bok'âta,' without adding any explanatory observation. Schumacher's el-Buk'âti would be in agreement if the feminine form with the termination i, usual in northern Palestine, is understood.—E. GUTHE.

square ; the tomb itself is covered with green silk cloth. An ancient infirm Sheikh watches over the sacred remains, and served us as a guide-book for the country. The Circassians bury around the Wely. On the northern crater girdle an easy much-frequented road leads to the large Circassian village, el·Breikeh, lying at the foot of the Tell ; and towards the west there are traces of old streets leading round the Tell to ej-Jueizeh and el-Breikeh. The view from the Tell rewards one. The Shâfet el-'Akkâsheh, in the south, is a portion of the old crater zone.

Tell el-Baiyâda (C. 1).—A mountain near Mejdel esh-Shems.

Tell el-Baram (D. 3).—A small characteristic volcano of circular form north of Tell el-'Urâm. Its crater is fairly well preserved ; oaks grow on its slopes.

Tell Bâzûk (C. D. 6).—An isolated hill above the debouch of the Wâdy Tell Bâzûk into the Joramâyeh, the slope and peak of which are covered with dolmens. The Wâdy Tell Bâzûk falls in vast high terraces from the plateau to the Joramâyeh. The precipitous walls of the gorge consist in part of column-shape basalt, which is continually hurled down and carried along as boulders. On the other hand, the river bed and lower walls, as much as 131 feet high, consist of limestone mixed with earthy substances. In summer a brook trickles down over the high precipices ; it is, however, dispersed on the rocks. It is said that in winter an imposing waterfall may be seen here.

Tell ed-Dara'îyeh (D. 5).—A portion of the crater wall of the el-Kuleiâh.

Tell edh-Dhahab (D. 6).—(*See* under Tell Abu el-Ghetâr.)

Tell el-Emhtr (E. 5).—(*See* under Tellul el-Asbah.)

Tell el-Faras (E. 5).—One of the most peculiar volcanoes of Jaulân, and which, as an isolated mountain, visible from a far distance, has been already frequently mentioned by travellers. Its highest point in the southeast reaches a height of 3,110 feet (above sea level, and 787 feet above the surrounding plain), and on this top is the unadorned Moslem tomb, the Makâm en-Neby Hasan ej-Jezzar, and a graveyard belonging to the Bedawîn. The oval crater of the Tell which is still very distinctly preserved, opens towards the north. Between the Makâm and the mouth of the crater the depth amounts to 108 feet. This latter has an opening of 18 feet by a depth of several feet ; the natives call it Mughârah (cave), and often dig there for supposed treasure. The crater walls fall regularly at an angle of 17° to 32°. The outer walls of the Tell, on the other hand, fall first steeply and then at an angle of 20° and 21°. Round the lowest part of the crater belt, especially in the north, there are distinct traces of a wall 3 feet in breadth, which may be followed in a circle for a length of about 525 feet, and perhaps served once as a protection to this lowest part. Or was the cauldron of the crater once used as a water reservoir (with the superstructure of the lower part) for the surrounding country? The slopes of the Tell are covered with lava slag; the ground is reddish-yellow. In the south there is a gentle hill; in the north-west a rocky crater wall lies before the Tell. The groups of small Tellûl el-Mallûl (2,965 feet) have probably arisen through its lava torrent flowing northward; their clayey, greasy, yellow soil is noticeably different from that of the Tellûl el-Humr, and their slopes are overgrown with oak underwood (Mallûl).

Tell el-Hâweh (C. 7).—Also called Tell el-Ferdâweh, an isolated hill on the debouch of the Rukkâd into the Yarmûk. It is covered with ruins. Walls of unhewn stones without mortar crown the summit; consequently the Tell was well fortified, and defended the entrance to both of the large river valleys.

Tell Krûm et-Turkoman (D.2).—The most northerly of the Tellul el-Bukâ'ti, 4,028 feet high (above sea level), and somewhat wooded. Its northern fissured and lacerated slopes fall towards the Birket Ram, and are covered with lava slag. The name recalls the first colonization of the Turkoman in this region.

Tell el-Mu'akkar (D. 6).—An isolated hill of the Zawîyeh east of the ruin el-Kuneitrah. Two wâdies called after it begin at its southern foot—one joins

with the Wâdy esh-Shebib ; the other, known also as
Seil el-Ghôr, joins with the Rukkâd.

Tell el-Muntar (C. 6).—The hill of the watch-tower
in the Zawiyeh, north of Kusr Bêrdawil, with a broad
basis, on whose peak we find ruins to which a tower
must have belonged. On the plain near are dolmens
and old building stones.

Tell esh-Sha'îr (B. 5).—A broad hill falling towards
the Batîhah ; it is somewhat cultivated.

Tell esh-Shebân (C. 3).—An isolated mountain, with
a demolished crater and oak trees, in the west of
Jaulân. Its peak (3,021 feet above sea level) is
crowned by the fallen-in square, Wely esh-Shebân,
the tomb of a Moslem saint. A few yards north the
Arab el-Fadel have buried those who fell in battle
against the Circassians, under a white plastered tomb,
visible from a far distance. A large, extremely deep,
round cistern is found near the Wely ; it holds rain-
water, and, like the Wely, must be very old. The
slopes of the Tell are covered with lava slag and
yellow soil ; the surrounding country is extraordinarily
stony.

Tell esh-Sheikhah (D. 2).—Certainly the highest of
all the volcanoes, its apex lying 4,245 feet above the
Mediterranean Sea ; it is, however, the least cha-
racteristic of them. It is the southern spur of the
Tellûl Bukâ'ti. Opposite the powerful Jebel esh-
Sheikh (Mount Hermon) it receives, as the slighter

elevation, the name Tell esh-Sheikhah (' Mountain of
the Old Woman ').

Tell es-Sikkeh (D. 6).—A large volcanic hill north-
east of Khisfîn, with ruins like those at Tell edh-
Dhahab.

Tell et-Taláyá (D. 5).—A long extended rocky hill
west of Tell el-Faras. Some trees and the Wely el-
Taláyá stand on its ridge (2,608 feet).

Tell el-Urâm (D. 3).—(*See* under Tell Abu en-
Nedá).

Tell Zahmûl (B. 3).—A hill overgrown with trees
on the Lake of Huleh.

Tell Zâkiyeh (C. 7).—A hill covered with ruins west
of el-'Âl. The large stones are mostly unhewn ; some
show hollows for the pivots of Haurân stone doors.
At the foot of the hill there is an old basalt oil
press-stone, 6½ feet in diameter.

Tell ez-Zátar (D. 3).—A hill peak on the western
slopes of Jaulân.

Tellul el-Asbah (E. 5).—Volcanic little hills near
Tell el-Faras, with traces of ruins on their summits.
The neighbouring Tell el-Emhîr is of the same nature
but without ruins. The Seil el-Emhîr is a rocky-
fissured river bed between this Tell and the foot of
the Tellul el-Hûmr, which in winter conveys water to
the Rukkâd.

Tellul el-Hûmr (E. 4, 5).—Two well-marked craters
near the Tell el-Faras. The western reaches a height of

S

3,319 feet, whilst the more easterly and wider is only 3,076 feet above the level of the sea. The slopes are covered with red soil, from which they get their name. Both craters open south, and are pretty well destroyed. The torrent of the eastern extends to the Rukkâd ; that of the western in an indistinct south-western direction.

Tellul es-S'âlib (properly *et-T'âlib,* ' Foxhill ') (B. 8). —A long low range of hills stretching from north to south, near the shore of the Lake of Tiberias, which is separated from the slopes of the Jaulân by the district Ben et-Tellûl. On its highest peak, which lies 305 feet above the level of the Sea of Galilee, or 377 feet below the Mediterranean Sea, we find a stone circle 22 feet in diameter, composed of rude blocks of basalt, towards the north, and round one terrace lower, a second larger one, 39 feet in diameter. The highest and most beautiful peak is called by the people Rujm et-Tell, and may have served as a signal point between the fort ed-Duêr and Tiberias. Continuing from here along the western margin of the hill down to es-Samra, one perceives along it a foundation 3 feet strong, with diagonal walls attaching, which are constructed of basalt blocks without mortar, and probably served as a protection to the small plateau of this hill, likewise occupied by square ruins. Presumably, therefore, there is an old site on Tellûl es-S'âlib.

Tlíl (C. 8).—A ruin with destroyed winter huts on the western slopes of the Wâdy Masâûd.

Et-Tu'enni (C. 7).—Some winter huts, with a good spring, 'Ain es-Sîdr or 'Ain et-Tu'enni. On the upper southern margin of the Wâdy es-Semakh, old building stones are to be found.

El-'Ulleika (C. 4).—A winter village of the Turkoman, consisting of ten huts. It is situated on the Wâdy el-Ulleika, which is here only 25 to 40 feet deeper than the surrounding country ; but as the Wâdy Dabûra soon grows deeper and more rocky, only a few old remains are extant. The district is so plentifully provided with water that in the west the village is surrounded by a great accumulation of running water, which it is not advisable to ride through. Fields of Italian corn, thereby irrigated, yield a good crop. Opposite the village, on the other side of the valley, on the viâ maris, lies the beautifully built cupola kind of Wely of the Sheikh Marzûk. The whitewashed building serves as a land-mark for a long distance. The tomb is supposed to contain the remains of the Saint and some of his relatives ; close by is a graveyard.

Umm el-'Ajaj (B. 5).—A small ruin on the slopes of the Batîhah, near which the Wely Umm el-'Ajaj stands.

Umm ed-Danânîr (D. 5).—District and hill near ed-Danurîyeh.

S 2

Umm el-Gheiyar (C. 3).—A winter village of the Turkoman, containing eight wretched huts, with few traces of building. The Bir el-Umm Gheiyar, a moderate sized spring, lies somewhat west of the village.

Umm el-Jehiyeh (C.7).—A village south of the Wâdy es-Semakh, on the spring of the same name, which in winter propels an extremely primitive mill. There are a few old building remains.

Umm el-Kanâtir (C. 6).—An important ruin on the eastern slopes of the Wâdy esh-Shebib. It lies on a level plain or terrace, a little below the high plateau, consequently on a protected place, as well as one of ambush. In the south, a powerful spring flows out of the rock ; it has a trough-like enclosure, and is walled over by two arches, 16 feet high (Figs. 130 and 131).

Fig. 130.
Fountain at Umm el-Kanâtir.

The masonry of the spring extended to the lava

plateau lying above ; but has fallen in in the west, where it apparently joined further masonry. It consists of powerful blocks of basalt, having a length

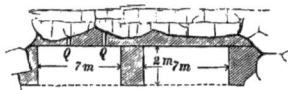

Fig. 131.
Plan of Fountain.

of 6½ feet by a thickness of 19 inches, and a height of 15 inches, which are carefully hewn and jointed, apparently without mortar. The archstones of the spring are arranged in the way shown on Fig. 132.

Fig. 132.
Portion of Arch.

The joints are only about one-fifth of an inch wide. Under one of the arches there lies an inscription tablet, whose signs are, however, entirely obliterated. Near here I dug a lion ornament out of the ground

(Fig. 133). Stepping northward over the source of
the spring, at a distance of 110 yards away, we come
upon a pile of ruins roofed with extraordinarily large

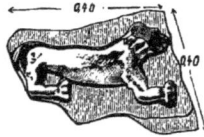

Fig. 133

basalt slabs, and probably graves might be found
underneath. It was here that the eagle ornament,
represented in Fig. 134, lay. Then we reach a large

Fig. 134.

rectangular building, 48 feet square, where carefully
hewn stones lie in gigantic piles upon one another,
concealing the bottom of the building; it is
believed that a stair running round the inner
room can be distinguished. Probably it was surrounded by a piazza similar to that found in ed-

Dikkeh ; the many fragments of basalt columns, having a diameter of 19 inches, which lie round beneath the ruins, incline one to this view. The entrance of the building (Fig. 135, A) is 6 feet wide.

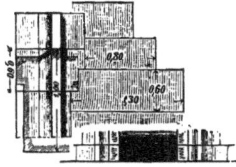

Fig. 135.

The courses and compilation of the stones near are and illustrated by Fig. 135. The joint lines are broken, the joints themselves are one-tenth of an inch wide, and mortarless ; the slabs used are of a quite unusual size, namely, 4 feet long by 23 inches in height, and 3 feet in thickness, the latter corresponding to the entire strength of the wall. The niche (Fig. 136) is

Fig. 136.

characteristic, also the base of a half column (Fig.

137), and, further, a curiously formed large stone

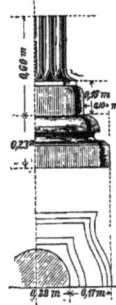

Fig. 137.

(Fig. 138), and the ornaments of Figs. 139 to 141.

Fig. 138.

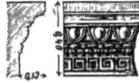

Fig. 139

Fig. 140.   Fig. 141.

As this ruin, so rich in profiles, is, however, lacking in any inscription, it is difficult to determine
the period of architecture. Its original name is evidently lost, because Umm el-Kanâtir only signifies
' Rich in arches.'

Umm el-Mutâbin (C. 7).—Destroyed Bedawîn huts,
with old building stones in Wâdy Semakh.

Wâdy Abu Hamâdah and *Wâdy Abûd* (C. 7) are
rocky side valleys of the Wâdy Fîk.

Wâdy el-'Ajam (D. E. 2).—The district bounding
the Jaulân on the north, a portion of Jedur.

Wâdy Barbârah (B. C. 7).—The western, and Wâdy
es-Sahûn, the eastern branch of the pleasant Wâdy
Masâûd.

Wâdy el-Barbûtîyeh (B. 6).—The name by which the
fishermen indicate the debouch of the Wâdy esh-
Shukeiyif into the Lake of Tiberias ; it is crowded
with fish.

Wâdy Batâh (C. 7, 8).—A deep narrow valley below
Dabbûseh, which unites with the Yârmûk.

Wâdy el-Halâwa (C. 3).—The upper part of the

Wâdy et-Tawâhîn, on the plain of Huleh. It begins
on the Ard el-Bâlûâ, but soon, however, dries up.

Wâdy el-Hamd (B. 3).—Called higher up Wâdy
Hafar. It absorbs the abundant 'Ain el-Tîneh, and
flows into the Lake of Huleh.

Wâdy Keleit (C. D. 8).—A large Wâdy of 'Ajlûn.

Wâdy el-Kiblêh (C. 2).—South of Za'ôra, leading
down to the Huleh marshes.

Wâdy Neskhtb (B. C. 6).—A broad partly cultivated
hollow in the plateau above the Batîhah, which in
winter is flooded.

Wâdy er-Rîh (B. C. 3).—A rocky and very fissured
valley, which leads down the slopes near er-Râwiyeh
into the Huleh plain.

Wâdy es-Saffâh, Wâdy ed-Dâlieh (B. 5,6), and *Wâdy
es-Senâm* are the three most important water-channels
of northern Batîhah, which, like the eastern Wâdy
Joramâyeh flood the plain in winter, but in summer
are more or less dried up.

Wâdy es-Samâr (C. 8).—A steep rocky wâdy near
'Ayûn, conveying some water, and discharging in the
Wâdy Masâûd.

Wâdy Sêisabân (A. 8).—The upper part of the
Ghôr and the Jordan, near the Lake of Tiberias.

Wâdyes-Semakh (C.6).—A valley*whose importance

---

* Ritter ('Erdkunde' xv., 1,287), according to De Bertou, states
" Wâdy es-Semak is a long valley which perforates the whole
system of chalk-mountains on the east coast separating it from

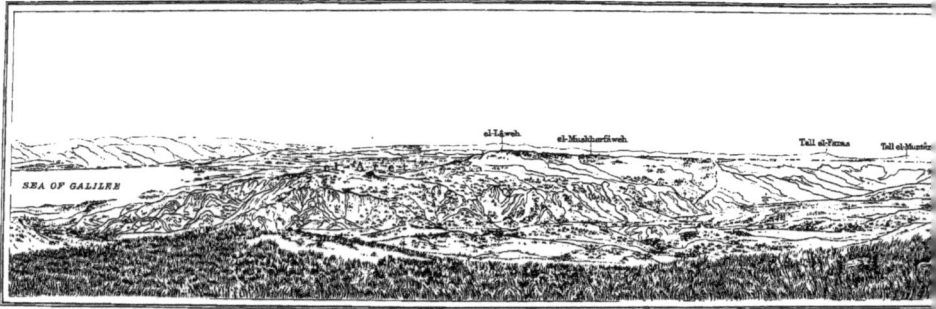

SEA OF GALILEE   el-Lāweh   el-Muakharfiweh   Tell el-Fazaa   Tell el-Muntiz

VIEW IN WADY ES-SEMAKH, FROM EL-AWANISH.
(from a Photograph)

for Jaulân has already been mentioned, and correctly
recognised by Seetzen and De Bertou (1839); and is,
indeed, of priceless significance for a plan of railway
and carriage roads. No other valley of the upper
Jordan land is suitable for this in an equal degree,
for all the others are either narrower, or have a too
precipitous crossing up the plateau.

The size or breadth of the Wâdy es-Semakh
amounts to 1½ miles. The outer margin of the valley
sides is encrusted with basalt lava, whilst chalky
slopes, especially in the south of the river bed itself,
fall quite gradually. A small stream gushes over the
valley bottom, which likewise consists of soft white
chalk rocks.

The length of the principal valley from the mouth
upwards is 4 miles. Then it contracts and divides
into two arms, the northern Wâdy esh-Shebîb
and the southern Wâdy ed-Diflch, with the Wâdy
el 'Âl. Both arms commence a little way from the
Tell Mu'akkar, and are precipitous and rocky, like all
other valleys of the Jaulân. In the principal valley,
which for civilising enterprises alone comes into consideration, there are many ruined places to be found,
a proof that the worth of this valley was already in

the Jaulân and the Haurân.   The Arabs name this cutting
the road of Haurân (Derb Hauran).   Wady es-Samak in a
future civilisation of this tract of country will be the most
important unloading place for Haurân."

earlier days recognised and turned to account. On
the southern slopes there is water, and to spare, and
the ground is very productive. Single oaks, bramble,
and other underwood, show that that wood growth
was at one period not lacking (*see* view of Wâdy
es-Semakh, from el-'Awanîsh).

Wâdy es-Sertr and *Wâdy es-Serts* (C. 6, 7).—Small
water channels on the southern slopes of the Wâdy
es-Semakh.

Wâdy esh-Sheikh-Ibrahîm (C. 5).—It begins near
the group of trees of the Wely esh-Sheikh-Ibrahîm not
far from Wahshara, and flows as the Wâdy es-Selba
into the Wâdy Yehûdiyeh. Its volume of water is
not inconsiderable.

Wâdy el-Washâsha (C. D. 4).—Further up Sei l'Ain
Eshsheh, a frightfully fissured and wild valley, which
joins with the Wâdy er-Ruzanîyeh.

Wakkâs (C. 8).—A small ruin with some Bedawîn
huts on a hill in Wâdy Masâûd. This name also recalls
the Wakûsa mountains occasionally mentioned in
the battle on the Yarmûk.

Washarah (C. 5).—A winter village of the Bedawîn,
with some ruins on a wâdy of the same name.

Wâsit (C. 3).—A shapeless ruin on the stony lava
district of Tell el-Urâm, near to which is a spring.

Wely Jâfer (C. 7).—The tomb of the wood saint of
Fik, with a beautiful terebinth.

El-Yâkûsah (C. 7).—A village consisting of 26 huts,

of which two in the south, built of stone and clay, are of remarkable size, and contain 120 inhabitants. On both sides the Wâdy es-Sahûn rises, being the upper rocky portion of the Wâdy Masâûd. The banks of the wâdy are rugged, the bed falls in terraces to a considerable depth, but widens below and gets pleasanter.* Some pomegranate trees adorn the village, which has otherwise a miserable appearance. The neighbourhood of el-Yâkûsah presents an unusual number of round and rectangular stone piles a few feet high, and enclosed by large unhewn blocks of rocks. The enclosed circle or square has a diameter of 6 to 10 feet and contains either a heap of carefully erected stones or is quite empty. In the last case we have probably remains of Bedawîn graves; on the other hand, in the former we are more reminded of the cromlechs or dolmen, although the characteristic basalt slabs and terrace formation are wanting here. Their design is most like the dolmens at Sheikh Khalet (*see* under Dolmens).

One of the most marked of these memorials is the

* Flugel, in his 'History of the Arabians,' p. 108, speaks on the occasion of the battle on the Yarmûk of "a valley sloping towards it which with its hill Wâkûsa form a gorge" into which the Byzantines were driven and lost. Probably this name is identical with the modern el-Yâkûsa, from which it differs only in the change of the initial letter. Then the valley would earlier have borne the name of the place Yakusa for all the channels of the rivers, almost without exception, even down to the present day, receive the name of the place they touch.

Rujûm el-Khiyar, south of el-Yâkûsah, close to its steep fall into the Yarmûk. The enclosing blocks of stone, reaching a cubic metre in size, are well filled up. The interior of the circle, which is 6½ feet high and 12 feet in diameter, is entirely filled up with large and small stones. Neither mortar nor any packing is to be discovered ; the joins of the masonry are distant and irregular, without, however, any detriment to the solidity of the structure. These stone heaps are generally erected on dominating points of the high plateau.

El-Yèhudiyeh (C. 5).—A large ruin on the Wâdy el-Yehudiyeh. On the north end two large newly-built corn magazines stand, which are only used during the harvest. The ruin lies on a narrow ridge, scarcely 220 yards wide, whose eastern slope is bounded by the depth of the perpendicular basalt rocks of the wâdy of the same name, whilst its western flank is bounded by a hollow, at its discharge into the Wâdy el-Yehudiyeh, but equally steep. The ridge runs over the junction of the two valleys to an acute triangle, upon the sharp edges of which a strong wall or tower, whose direction can be traced with but few interruptions round the entire ruin. These stones are rude and fitted together without mortar and form powerful walls, 6 feet in thickness, on the less protected western side, in contradistinction to walls of slight thickness on the side which is inaccessible

by nature. In the north the mountain ridge widens
to a plateau, upon which there are indistinct traces
of the kind described, whereas remains of former
buildings on a square plan are still to be found. The
chamber enclosed by the wall is covered with ruins
of all kinds ; most of all one sees large hewn basalt
building stones, lying in heaps near greatly weather-
worn shafts of columns. Besides these, most peculiar
capitals (Figs. 142 and 143) are to be found, which

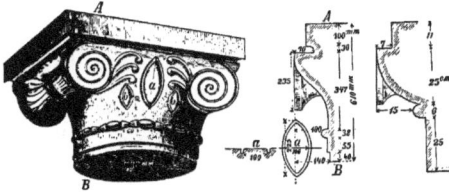

Fig. 142.

Capital at el-Yehudîyeh.

Fig. 143.

Section of Capital.

exhibit a very primitive application of the combined
Ionic and Corinthian styles. These are already very
weather-worn, and like the other ruins point to a great
age. Near the column remains two well preserved top
stones lie ; they are of the same shape and still in
their original position, opposite one another (Fig. 144).
If the ruins on the surface are not important, they at

any rate exhibit characteristic construction and peculiar forms found nowhere else in the Jaulân. Excavations will certainly bring to light more important
discoveries, and by this means yield information as to

Fig. 144.

Top-stone at el-Yehudîyeh.

whether el-Yehudîyeh, its name and tradition, are of
Jewish origin or not. I was unfortunately unable to
examine the inner of the two corn magazines, as the
openings were barricaded. According to the statements of the natives, inscriptions were found below
the ruins, but no one could tell me where these were
lost.

Zakîyeh (B. 6).—The name of the bay indenting
into the Batîhah ; the water is uncommonly slimy and
dirty.

Za'ôra (C. 2).—A well built Nusairier village in the
northern extremity of the Jaulân, making a cresent
round the fall of the slope. It comprises 65 huts with
about 350 persons, who consequently live close together.
They cultivate the Huleh marshes with rice, and the
country round the village with famous tobacco. The

roofs of the houses bear huts made of branches or poles. The village itself has no living water, but several old cisterns. The Sheikh is supposed to have discovered an old aqueduct at the slope, where in winter a small stream gushes forth. The old building stones lying round do not, however, afford any certain confirmation of this assertion. The nearest spring is 'Ain Fît. To the east a huge old terebinth stands shading a decayed Moslem tomb, called el-'Adjami. Otherwise, Za'ôra possesses very few remains of antiquity.

Ez-Zârûra (C. 3).—A rocky district and a Bedawîn graveyard near er-Râwiyeh, with a Zárûr bush (white thorn) the last remnant of a large thicket.

Zeita (C. 6).—A small Bedawîn village with some ruins, in the neighbourhood of the Wâdy Joramâyeh.

Zôr en-Nîs, Zôr Ramadan, Zôr Abu Kubzeh* (C. 8), *or Zôr er-Riyâs* (D. 7) are collections of rock projections with small basalt terraces on the Yarmûk.

---

* Zôr en Nîs, Zôr Ramadan, or Zôr Abu Kubzeh.

INDEX TO THE NAMES.

T 2

Transliteration.	Arabic.	Translation.	Page.
'Arab el Huwâj	عرب الحواج		169
'Arab ej Jeâtîn	عرب الجعاتين		87
'Arab el Kefarât	عرب الكفرات		88
'Arab el Menâdireh	عرب المناضرة		{ 88 D 7
'Arab el Mukhaibeh	عرب المخيبه		88
'Arab en Neârneh	عرب النعرنى		89
'Arab en Nùêm (el Yùsef)	عرب النعيم (اليوسف)		89
'Arab er Rekêbât	عرب الرقيبات		90
'Arab es Sebârdjah	عرب السبارجة		135
'Arab es Siyâd	عرب السيّاد		91
'Arab et Tellawîyeh	عرب التلّوية		91
'Arab Turkoman Teljeh	عرب تركمان تلجة		91
'Arab el Weslyeh	عرب الويسيّة		92
el 'Araj	العرج		93
'Arâk el Ahmar	عراق الاحمر	Red Height	93
*'Arâk el 'Arrâbeh	عراق العرّابة	Height (Edge) of the Godmother (Sch.)	93
'Arâk Abu Jedeiyeh	عراق ابو يديّة		93
'Arâk Rakâkiya	عراق ركاكية		229
Ard el 'Alâ	ارض العلا	Country of the Heights	94
Ard el Bâlûâ	ارض البالوعة	Land of the Precipice	94
Ard el Ekhdeiyil	ارض الغديّل		95

Transliteration.	Arabic.	Translation.	Page.
el Khôka	الخوخة	Plum Tree	186
Kh. 'Ain el Hôr	خربة عين الحور	Ruined placed of the White Poplar Spring	186
Kh. el 'Arâis	خربة العرائس	Ruins of the Bride	187
Kh. el 'Âshek	خربة العاشق	Ruin Places of the Beloved	187
Kh. 'Atâr Ghazâl	خربة آثار غزال	Ruined Place of the traces of the Gazelle	187
Kh. el Batrah	خربة البترة		188
Kh. ed Durdâra	خربة الدردارة	Ruins of the Elm (Ash)	188
Kh. Jiât	خربة جياة		188
Kh. Jort ed Dhahab	خربة جورة الذهب	Ruined Places of the Gold Mine	189
Kh. Kôdana	خربة كودنة	Ruined Places of the (ignoble) Horse	189
Kh. el Mêdân	خربة الميدان	Ruin Places of the Open Space	191
Kh. el Mudowarah	خربة المدوّرة	The Round Ruins	191
Kh. Mukâtyeh	خربة مكاتية		191
Kh. el Mukhfy	خربة المنخفى		192
Kh. Sakûkeh	خربة سكوكه		192
Kh. esh Shareireh	خربة الشريرة		193
Kh. Sîhân	خربة سيحان		193
el Khushnîyeh	الخشنيّة		194
Kisrîn	قصرين		194

Transliteration.	Arabic.	Translation.	Page.
Makâm el Yáfûreh	مقام اليعفورى		D 2
Makht. el 'Adesîyeh	مخاضة العديسيّة		218
Makhâd Esbêh	مخاض صبيح		218
*Makht. el Ikful	مخاضة القفول	The Ford of the Caravans	218
Makht. el Mareiyeh	مخاضة المرعيّة		218
Makht. es Seiyarah	مخاضة السيّارة		218
Makht. Umm Kharrubeh	مخاضة امّ خروبة		218
Makht. Umm Sherûb	مخاضة امّ الشروب		218
Makran el Widiân	مقرن الوديات	Junction of the Valley Beds	218
Mamid el Ma'ánek	ممد المعانق		218
el Mansûrah (1)	المنصورة		218
el Mansûrah (2)			218
el Medjâmiá	المجامع		219
el Medjnûneh	المجنونة	The Crazy Woman	220
el Mejdelîyeh	المجدليّة		220
Merj el Buk'âti	مرج البقاعة		{ 12 { 252
Merj el Ekseir	مرج القصار		134
Merj ej Jiât	مرج الجيّاة	Meadow, Meadowland of	189
*Merj el Katreineh	مرج القطرانى		78
Merj et Tabel	مرج الطبل	Drum Meadow	220
Merj el Yáfûreh	مرج اليعفورى		220

U

Transliteration.	Arabic.	Translation.	Page.
er Rafîd	الرفيد		{ 226-229
*Rakâkiyah	ركاكية		229
*Rân Jîbîn	ران جبين	Trough ? of Jibîn	163
Râs 'Ain el Bêdâ	رأس عين البيضاء		79
*Râs el 'Akabeh	رأس العقبة	Summit of the Ascent	182
Râs el Hâl	رأس البحال		229
Râs esh Shââf	رأس الشعاف		239
Râs esh Sheikhah	رأس الشقيحة		229
*Râs Tawâfik	رأس توافيق		245
Rasm el Hîrân	رسم الحيران		229
er Râwiyeh	الراوية	The Water Bottle or Pipe	{ 125 229
Rôd el Bâneh	روض البان		230
er Ruhîneh	الروحينة		230
Rujum el 'Abdeh	رجم العبدة	Stone-heap of the Female Slave	230
Rujum el 'Abhar	رجم البهر	Stone-heap of the Styrax.	230
Rujum Abu Mashâk	رجم ابو مشاق	Stone-heap of A.M.	230
Rujum el Butm	رجم البطم	Stone-heap of the Terebinths	230
Rujum el Fâr	رجم الفار	Stone-heap of the Mice	230
Rujum el Khiyâr	رجم الخيار		231
Rujum et Tell			258

Transliteration.	Arabic.	Translation.	Page.
Shâfet 'Ain Eshsheh	شعفة عين عشّة	Top of the Nest-spring	76
Shâfet Esbéh	شعفات صبح		218
Shâfet Kutta	شعفات قطة		239
Shâfet es Sindiâneh	شعفة السنديانة	The summit of the Stone Oak	{ 15 / 239 }
esh Shârah	الشعرة		{ 9 / 62 / 176 }
*Sheffet esh el Ghorâb	شفّة عش الغراب		239
*Sheffet Môbarah	شفّة موبرة	The Edge of the ...	{ 12 / 236 }
*Sheffet Tabak el Melâweh	شفّة طبق الملاوى		240
esh Sheikh 'Abdullah	شيخ عبدالله		246
Sheikh Faiyad 'Abd el Ghaneh	شيخ فيّاض ابد الغنى		138
Sheikh Ahsen			C 5
esh Sheikh Khalil	الشيخ خليل		240
Sheikh Marzûk	شيخ مرزوق		259
Sheikh Muhammed	شيخ محمد		160
Sheikh el Mukhfy	شيخ المخفى		192
esh Sheikh Mûsâ	الشيخ موسى	The Sheikh Moses	96
Sheikh Rajâl	شيخ رجل		169
esh Sheikh Shehadeh el Fadl	الشيخ شهادة الفضل		87
Shejeret el 'Ajami	شجرة العجمى	The Tree of the Persian (Strangers)	D 7
Shejeret el 'Ameri	شجرة العمرى		240

Transliteration.	Arabic.	Translation.	Page.
Summâka	سماقة	The Somach Plant	242
es Sûr	السور	The Wall	190
Sûrramân (Surr el Mâl)	سرمان (سر المال)		243
Sûsiyeh	سوسية		244
es Sûwâneh	الصوّانة	The Flint	244
Suweihîyah	سويهية		244
Tâhûnet el Ulleikah	طاحونة العليقة	Mill of the Black-berry Bushes	244
Taket el Harîreh	طاقة الحريرة		222
Tât Ahsein	طاة حسين		245
Tawâfîk	توافيق		245
Têlestân	طيلستان		245
et Tell	التل	The Hill	245
Tell Abu el Ghêtâr	تل ابو الغيطار		246
Tell Abu ej Jaj	تل ابو دجاج		247
Tell Abu Katif	تل ابو قطف		247
Tell Abu el Khánzír	تل ابو الخنزير		{ 15 247
Tell Abu Kubeis	تل ابو كبيس		247
Tell Abu en Nedâ	تل ابو الندى		{ 14 247
Tell Abu Yûsef	تل ابو يوسف		{ 14 251
Tell Abu Zeitûneh	تل ابو زيتونة		252
Tell el Ahmar	تل الاحمر	The Red Hill	{ 15 252

Transliteration.	Arabic.	Translation.	Page.
Tell el 'Akkâsheh	تلّ العكّاشة		252
Tell el Baiyâda	تلّ البيّاضة		253
Tell el Baram	تلّ البرم		{ 14 253
Tell Bârûk	تلّ بازوك		253
Tell ed Darâîyeh	تلّ الدرعيّة		254
Tell edh Dhahab	تلّ الذهب	Gold Hill	254
Tell el Ehdeib	تلّ الهديب		35
Tell el Emhîr	تلّ المهير	Hill of the Little Foal	254
ell el Faras	تلّ الفرس	Hill of the Horses	254
Tell el Ferdâweh or Tell el Haweh	تلّ الفرداوى	The Isolated ? Hill	255
Tell el Ferj	تلّ الفرج		136
Tell el Fizâra	تلّ الفزارة		146
Tell el Hâweh	تلّ الحاف	Hill of the Serpent Tamers	35
Tell ej Jiât	تلّ جياة		189
Tell Jôkhadâr	تلّ جوخادار		184
Tell Krûm et Turkoman	تلّ كروم التركمان	Hill of the Vineyards of the Turkomen	255
Tell Mu'akkir	تلّ معكّر		255
Tell el Muntâr	تلّ المنطار	Hill of the Watch Tower	256

Transliteration.	Arabic.	Translation.	Page.
Umm el 'Ajâj	ام العجاج	The Smoky, dusty (?)	259
Umm ed Danânîr	ام الدنانير	Possessor, denaric	{ 118, 259, 265
el Umm Gheiyar	المغيّر		C 3
el Umm Jehîyeh	المجهيّة	The fallen in or fallen down (Schum).	C 7
Umm el Kanâtir	ام القناطر	Possessing arches	265
Umm el Mutâbin	ام المتابن	Magazines with chopped straw	265
*Wâdy Abu Hamâdah	وادى ابو حمادة		265
*Wâdy 'Abûd	وادى عبود		265
Wâdy el 'Ajam	وادى العجم	(District)	9, 265
Wâdy el 'Âl	وادى العال		267
Wâdy el 'Amûdîyeh	وادى العموديّة		C 5
*Wady 'Ayûn	وادى عيون	Spring Valley	222
Wâdy 'Ain el Ghazâleh	وادى عين الغزالة	Valley of the Gazelle Spring	77
*Wâdy Barbâreh	وادى بربارا		265
Wâdy el Barbûtîyeh	وادى البربوطيّة		265
Wâdy Batâh	وادى بطاح		265
Wâdy Bâzûk	وادى بازوك		253
Wâdy Bêdârûs			241
*Wâdy Bîr el Kabak	وادى بئر الكبك		215
*Wâdy el Bîreh	وادى البيرة		237
Wâdy Dabûra	وادى دبوره		119
Wâdy ed Dalieh	وادى الداليّة	Vine Valley	266

Names of the Bedawîn Tribes who winter in the
Jaulân according to the Official Register.

Transliteration.	Arabic.	Number of Tents (5 persons to a Tent.)
'Arab el-Abu 'Asî	عرب الابو عاصى	6
'Arab el-Abu 'Eid	عرب الابو عيد	12
'Arab Abu 'Eid Hameideh	عرب ابو عيد حميدك	8
'Arab el-Abu Hajâ	عرب الابو حيا	30
'Arab Ahmed esh-Shibleh	عرب احمد الشبلى	6
'Arab el-'Akeidât	عرب العقيدات	300
'Arab el-Bakkâr	عرب البكار	90
'Arab Beni Nimr	عرب بنى نمير	120
'Arab Beni Rabi'a	عرب بنى ربيعة	40
'Arab ed-Dheiwât	عرب الدهيوات	4
'Arab el-Hadâideh	عرب الجدايدة	8
'Arab el-Hamâmra	عرب الجماءرة	45
'Arab Harb	عرب حرب	120
'Arab Jallâli Wa-'azi	عرب جلالى وعزى	16
Arab ej-Jamaileh	عرب الجمايلة	45
'Arab el-Kabaireh	عرب الكبايرة	10

Transliteration.	Arabic.	Number of Tents (5 persons to a Tent.)
'Arab el-Manâfeh	عرب المنافى	8
'Arab el-Merâzka	عرب المرازقا	50
'Arab en-Nu 'eimât et-Tâ'a	عرب النعيمات الطاعة	35
'Arab er-Ramla	عرب الرملة	30
'Arab es-Seikât	عرب الصيكات	4
'Arab Shâm	عرب شأم	8
'Arab esh-Sharâhleh	عرب الشراحلى	30
'Arab et-Tahaineh	عرب الطهاينة	12
'Arab Turkoman Suweidîyeh	عرب تركمان سوادِيّة	18
'Arab el-Umhammadat	عرب المحمّدات	6
'Arab el-'Utba	عرب العتبة	22
'Arab el-Wâsit	عرب الواسط	45
'Arab Wesiyet el-Gharâba	عرب ويسِيّة الغرابا	20

THE END.

HARRISON AND SONS, PRINTERS IN ORDINARY TO HER MAJESTY, ST. MARTIN'S LANE, LONDON.